# GETTING
## ALONG
*Famously*

For Sara —
A great business partner
and a great friend . . .
All the best,

Melissa Hellstern

ALSO BY MELISSA HELLSTERN

How to Be Lovely:
The Audrey Hepburn Way of Life

# GETTING ALONG FAMOUSLY

## A Celebration
### OF Friendship

MELISSA HELLSTERN

DUTTON

Published by Penguin Group (USA) Inc.

375 Hudson Street, New York, New York 10014, U.S.A.

Penguin Group (Canada), 90 Eglinton Avenue East, Suite 700, Toronto, Ontario M4P 2Y3, Canada (a division of Pearson Penguin Canada Inc.); Penguin Books Ltd, 80 Strand, London WC2R 0RL, England; Penguin Ireland, 25 St Stephen's Green, Dublin 2, Ireland (a division of Penguin Books Ltd); Penguin Group (Australia), 250 Camberwell Road, Camberwell, Victoria 3124, Australia (a division of Pearson Australia Group Pty Ltd); Penguin Books India Pvt Ltd, 11 Community Centre, Panchsheel Park, New Delhi – 110 017, India; Penguin Group (NZ), 67 Apollo Drive, Rosedale, North Shore 0632, New Zealand (a division of Pearson New Zealand Ltd); Penguin Books (South Africa) (Pty) Ltd, 24 Sturdee Avenue, Rosebank, Johannesburg 2196, South Africa

Penguin Books Ltd, Registered Offices: 80 Strand, London WC2R 0RL, England

Published by Dutton, a member of Penguin Group (USA) Inc.

First printing, October 2008

10   9   8   7   6   5   4   3   2   1

 REGISTERED TRADEMARK—MARCA REGISTRADA

LIBRARY OF CONGRESS CATALOGING-IN-PUBLICATION DATA

has been applied for.

ISBN 978-0-525-95080-6

Printed in the United States of America

Set in Bembo

Designed by Susan Hood

For my parents—

Mom, Dad and Cindy—

who I am very lucky to also call my friends.

# Contents

# Introduction

A friend is someone who knows the
song in your heart and can sing it back
to you when you have forgotten the
words.

—ANONYMOUS

In mathematics, the butterfly effect says that a storm in New England may be caused by a butterfly flapping its wings in China. The world is so sensitive a place, so connected, the smallest act can change things forever. Friendship is the same way—sometimes we do not know how important a first meeting is. One chance meeting may, with time, lead to a friendship that keeps you laughing, feeds your mind or makes even the worst day feel easier. Friendship can sustain you.

If you want to get primitive about it, remember that as

gatherers, cooperation among women was vital to survival. We, quite literally, needed our friends to go on living. The same can be said in today's urban jungle. Studies have shown that having at least one close confidant can improve your longevity and reduce the risk of physical impairments as you age. It has even been said that living without close friends can be as bad for your health as smoking or being overweight.

With my friends, I have danced the night away in a Florence disco, learned to speak French, drunk too many martinis, survived bad relationships, taken kickboxing, toppled a canoe, explored art, read new books, driven cross-country, found the perfect dress, cooked a turkey, ridden horseback up a mountain, sung in a choir, gone skydiving and understood life lessons. Along the way, I have shared my hopes, my dreams, my experiences and my heart. And been made better for having done so.

Friendship makes us better women, better lovers and better mothers. When we play together, laugh together or cry together, we bring more meaning into our lives. Men may fix things, but women fix each other. When a friend says "yes, you can" or "it will get better" or "his loss," you know it is true.

If we are smart, we choose our friends based on the things that really matter—loyalty, an offbeat sense of humor, shared interests or a listening ear. My friends lift me up when I am down, laugh at the absurd and love me through it all. When one of us goes down a pant size, we all celebrate. If a man disappoints us, we rally together. In crucial moments, we can make major life decisions over a cup of coffee.

My grandfather once said, "You are lucky to have ten true friends in your lifetime." The older I get, the more his words ring true. Marriage, children, careers—life can get awfully busy. And friendship takes time, generosity, unconditional love and support.

Real friendship will transcend any distance, any lifestyle change and any amount of time. I have friends I speak to every day, some I chat with every week and others I catch up with only once a year. Yet these bonds are equally important. For I know that any one of them would be there for me in a second if I needed her.

The beauty of friendship is that in the long run, it will likely outlast romantic relationships. And since women generally outlive men, sticking together can really pay off. With all that said, friendship can sometimes be hard to define. It is a fickle, subjective and elusive experience. Why is she my friend? Because she just is. Still, one thing is certain: sharing the journey—the highs and lows—makes it all that much sweeter.

*Audrey Hepburn*
*and*
*Sophia Loren*

Chapter One

# Friends
# share pasta

When Audrey Hepburn came on the scene, director Billy Wilder said, "This girl, single-handedly, may make bosoms a thing of the past." At the time, the curves of Sophia Loren were so steaming up the screen that she was known as the "Italian Marilyn Monroe."

Audrey and Sophia have their husbands to thank for bringing them together. In 1955, Carlo Ponti—Sophia's husband—and his producing partner, Dino De Laurentiis, decided to bring Tolstoy's epic novel *War and Peace* to the big screen. Newlyweds Audrey and Mel Ferrer signed on to play the lead roles.

On the surface it may seem an incongruent pairing—the gamine good girl and the sexy screen siren—yet Audrey and Sophia had much in common. With a similar outlook on life, love and fame, they were girlfriends who cooked together, walked together and shared all the highs and lows.

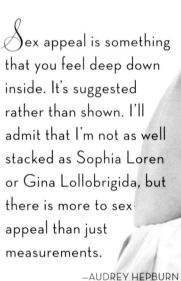

$\mathcal{S}$ex appeal is something that you feel deep down inside. It's suggested rather than shown. I'll admit that I'm not as well stacked as Sophia Loren or Gina Lollobrigida, but there is more to sex appeal than just measurements.

—AUDREY HEPBURN

## LITTLE WOMEN

From the beginning, both Audrey and Sophia were unlikely stars. As a child, Sophia was considered something of an ugly duckling (her nickname was *stechetto*, Italian for "the stick"), while Audrey was notoriously quiet and introverted. No one would have predicted that Hollywood would bring them together.

In Sophia, Audrey found her independent, self-aware counterpart. Raised by strong, single mothers, Audrey and Sophia were taught to be resourceful and self-sufficient. Sophia's parents never married, while Audrey's parents divorced early on. And both mothers were stage mothers in the making. When their own personal hopes of being actresses were dashed, they became driving forces in their daughters' careers, living vicariously through their triumphs.

Audrey was Dutch, Sophia Italian. Sophia famously said she had two big advantages at birth—to have been born wise and to have been born into poverty. And though Audrey's mother had a title—baroness—she did not have the wealth to go along with it.

Their childhoods were also robbed by the realities of war. Living near starvation and without opportunity replaced their childhood innocence with a wisdom beyond their young years. Yet it was growing up during World War II that gave them a tremendous sense of gratitude for everything that came after.

Their childhoods made them equally humble, down-to-earth and focused on the things that really matter—family, food and safety.

"It made me resilient and terribly appreciative for everything good that came afterward," Audrey said. "I felt enormous respect for food, freedom, for good health and family—for human life."

These humble beginnings provided just the basis that made them if not wise to the ways of Hollywood, at least less susceptible to them. "All my career, all my life, I've had to fight back hard—particularly in my private life," Sophia would later say. "Each time, I won, but from the beginning, I had to fight just for food and shelter, so the roof over my head is sacred to me."

*Friendship is born at that moment when one person says to another: "What! You, too? Thought I was the only one."*

*C. S. Lewis*

## THE MALE SPECIES

Early in their careers, Audrey and Sophia both relied heavily on their spouses. Perhaps being raised without a strong father figure left both women longing for a protective male companion. When it came to men, Audrey and Sophia seemed to be drawn to the same qualities—and it had nothing to do with what was on the outside.

Not terribly long after her first big film and her first Oscar, Audrey met producer/director/actor Mel Ferrer. Nearly twelve years her senior and thrice divorced, Mel inspired in Audrey a passion that outweighed the accusations made by the press. He was not her Svengali, she said, just her loving husband. "The kind of man I'm attracted to can be tall or short, fair or dark, handsome or homely," Audrey said. "Physical good looks don't necessarily appeal to me just by themselves. If a man has that indefinable quality that I can only call 'warmth' or 'charm,' then I'll feel at ease with him."

Sophia had producer Carlo Ponti, whom she had known since the

# Side by Side

[Sophia] was a very large girl with gaps between her front teeth and a red dress gathered in a sash on one splendid hip. Standing with Audrey, who was tall and slender as a boy, they looked two different species, and both of them collector's items.

—BRITISH DIRECTOR MICHAEL POWELL, ON SEEING AUDREY AND SOPHIA TOGETHER AT A DINNER PARTY

tender age of sixteen. More than twenty years her senior, Carlo had been a judge in the Miss Roma contest Sophia had entered. While Sophia placed only second in the contest, Carlo would always come first. They made something of an odd couple—he was much shorter than she and balding—but he soon became her manager and eventually her husband. "For me, what really counts is his intelligence: his thoughts, his chosen way of being," Sophia said. "I never just look at a man's exterior. I may notice, in a very abstract way, that he's handsome or has nice eyes, but that isn't how he strikes me as a man or attracts me as a woman. It takes more than that to awaken my interest. If he's very well dressed, well, so is furniture."

# SWISS MISSES

For a time, Audrey and Sophia were neighbors. Far from the glare of Hollywood, Switzerland was a refuge from the demands of being a star and, most importantly, from the press. Here they shared long country walks, quiet confidences and casual dinners in the kitchen while their husbands were away.

Audrey came to Switzerland in 1954 for some much-needed rest and relaxation. Speaking about Burgenstock, a small alpine village perched high on a mountain overlooking Lake Lucerne, Audrey said, "I love to wake up early in the morning, throw open the shutter and drink in the sight of the tall mountain peaks and the lake down below." Soon after, she and Mel were married there. From that point forward, no matter where she traveled, Switzerland would always be home.

Though she would eventually move from Burgenstock to Tolochenaz-sur-Morges, Switzerland was always where Audrey felt most herself. "I love it. I love the country. I love our little town. The shops. I love going to the open market twice a week with all the fruit and vegetables and flowers. . . . It is because I live in the country in Switzerland that I can lead a totally unselfconscious life and be totally myself."

Not long after, Sophia and Carlo came to Switzerland for a different reason. In 1957, they were having trouble getting their marriage recognized by the very Catholic Italian government. And they hoped Switzerland might just offer the right

solution: new citizenship. Perhaps it was even Audrey's idea.

> *Sex appeal is fifty percent what you've got and fifty percent what people think you've got.*
>
> —SOPHIA LOREN

To be remarried, Carlo needed to annul his marriage to his first wife. With the Vatican not keen to recognize his Mexican divorce, his subsequent Mexican wedding to Sophia made him a bigamist. To avoid a lengthy jail term, the Mexican divorce and remarriage had to be annulled, leaving Sophia bereft of living as a proper wife to the man she loved. "I give up," Sophia said. "I'm married, I'm not married. I'm this, I'm that. *Basta.* I feel married, and lots of married people don't feel married."

The couple lived abroad—and sometimes secretly in Italy— until 1966, when they became French citizens and were able to be married there. "When the law in Italy was persecuting Carlo and me as criminals guilty of bigamy, the marriage of Audrey Hepburn and Mel Ferrer seemed to me like a dream— far away and unreachable. . . . In those days she was so happy, she inspired my dream [of the same]."

# WHO IS THE MOST BEAUTIFUL WOMAN YOU KNOW?

" Carole Bouquet, because she is undoubtedly beautiful—and she is one of my best friends. Women who *stay true to themselves* are always more interesting and beautiful to me. Women like Frida Kahlo, Georgia O'Keeffe and Anna Magnani. Women who have style, chic, allure and elegance. They didn't submit to any standard of beauty—they defined it. "

—ISABELLA ROSSELLINI

" I would rather see her smoke a cigarette than spend a day in a museum. She smokes it with passion, humor, grace and hunger. To watch Simone is a joy—the actress, the complete woman *involved* in the exciting business of living. "

—ROSALIND RUSSELL
ON HER FRIEND SIMONE SIGNORET

*I* like to talk to very close friends about feelings, but I hate chatter.

—AUDREY HEPBURN

## ACTING UP

When it came to their careers, Audrey and Sophia made their marks with a devout work ethic, plenty of pluck and a practicality that would carry them through most any situation. Sophia once said, "Whatever I ask of life is something life can give me. I never sought the impossible dream, but from life I sometimes got the impossible dream because I took it step by step, little by little, with patience, too. If you wait for the impossible dream to come true, it won't. But if you work at a little corner of it and then another corner, well, one day you may have the whole mosaic."

For all their acting accomplishments, neither Audrey nor Sophia had had any classical training. They acted by instinct as much as anything. Sophia explained, "My technique consists simply of following my basic instincts. The actress in me is only released the moment the camera demands it. The word 'Action!' frees me. I kick away self-consciousness and I feel liberated, uninhibited, even reckless. The transformation is something I cannot explain. It is fragile and mysterious, and too much analysis might destroy it."

For her part, Audrey said, "I never really became an actress—in the sense that when people ask me how I did it, my only answer is 'I wouldn't know.' I just walked on the set knowing my lines and took it from there."

Though they never appeared on-screen together, they did

occasionally cross paths in their professional lives. After working with Audrey on *War and Peace*, Carlo proposed making Chekhov's *Three Sisters* with Sophia, Audrey and Ingrid Bergman, but he failed to get the green light from Paramount. In 1964, Mel worked alongside Sophia in the all-star epic *The Fall of the Roman Empire*.

In 1962, both women were nominated for an Academy Award for Best Actress. Audrey for *Breakfast at Tiffany's*— perhaps her most iconic role—and Sophia for *Two Women*, the harrowing story of a woman trying to protect her teenage daughter from the horrors of war. Because of her great respect for Audrey's talent, Sophia was sure that Audrey would win, and decided not to travel to the United States to attend the ceremony. No doubt she was surprised when she made Oscar history that night—hers was the first foreign-language performance to be honored by the academy. Cary Grant, a friend of both women, called her to share the good news.

Later in their careers, Audrey and Sophia would both go on to win Grammys in the category Best Spoken Word Album for Children. Audrey won with *Audrey Hepburn's Enchanted Tales* in 1993, and Sophia ten years later, in 2003, for *Prokofiev: Peter and the Wolf / Beintus: Wolf Tracks*.

## APRON STRINGS

Homebodies through and through, Audrey and Sophia relished the pleasures of domesticity. While it's hard to imagine either of them cleaning the bathroom, certainly they loved to cook for family and friends. The perfect evening was similar for each—a quiet dinner, television and an early bedtime. And pasta was the meal of choice. "Spaghetti can be eaten most successfully if you inhale it like a vacuum cleaner," Sophia once said. Imagine two of the world's leading ladies inhaling pasta in the kitchen.

Food was both a privilege to be indulged in and a pleasure to be enjoyed. Sophia was such a good cook that she wrote

two charming cookbooks, entitled *In the Kitchen with Love* and *Sophia Loren's Recipes and Memories*. In one introduction, she says, "No delicacies or frills can make food as appetizing as an empty belly can. Those of us who were children during the Second World War can bear prime witness to this great truth. Hunger—real, visceral hunger—forced us to face many dangers in those years, but it also gave us great courage, and even today I remain in awe of what we experienced."

Audrey was known for her self-indulgent trips to the market, where no gastronomic pleasure was denied. "When you have had the strength to survive starvation," Audrey said, "you never again send back a steak simply because it's underdone."

Cooking and its simple pleasures were not only about food, but also about the worlds they both felt very lucky to have. "The main thing to be doing is to nourish yourself and to nourish each other," Sophia has said. "I'm not just talking about food but about marriage, motherhood, movies, relationships, retirement, everything. And you have to work at every single thing. Life is work. Without ever realizing it, you're working at life every day."

After all, how many good friends can you have in life? Four or five. The rest are just acquaintances you meet at a party.

—SOPHIA LOREN

## VICES

Scotch and cigarettes are not terribly in keeping with the public image of these two stars, yet they did sometimes indulge when relaxing at home. While Audrey once joked, "My mother taught to me to only smoke six cigarettes a day," she shared this vice with her friend Sophia. At the end of a typical day, Audrey was also known to pour herself two fingers of scotch. Sophia often ordered "scotch on the stones" because it always got the same laugh as when she first made the mistake.

# Grace Kelly and Josephine Baker

Grace was our real-life Cinderella, a regal actress who married a prince and reigned over Monaco. Josephine grew up dirt-poor and went on to become the queen of Parisian nightlife. Both were beautiful, talented American exports. The popular myth about their friendship goes that, when Josephine was denied service at New York's famed Stork Club due to her race, Grace took her by the arm and stormed out with her entire party in tow, vowing never to return.

Though the story is untrue (Grace was not there that night), the two women's friendship was real. Grace became an activist in support of charitable organizations and the arts, raising funds for the Red Cross, supporting mothers and children, and quietly funding artists she believed in. Josephine worked to abolish racial segregation, refusing to perform for segregated audiences and speaking at the 1963 March

on Washington next to Martin Luther King Jr. When Josephine—
who adopted twelve children of different ethnicities, which she
called her Rainbow Tribe—fell on hard times, it was Grace who
offered her lifelong accommodations in a home near Monaco.
Though retired, Josephine returned the favor by filling in at the last
minute for a missing Sammy Davis Jr. at Grace's gala for the Red
Cross—and earned a standing ovation. Grace was there when
Josephine staged her own Paris comeback at the age of sixty-eight.
Two days later, Josephine was found in a coma surrounded by the
rave reviews from her show. She was the first
American woman to receive full French military
honors. Her Paris funeral was attended by
more than twenty thousand people, many of
them heads of state. She is interred at the
cemetery in Monaco.

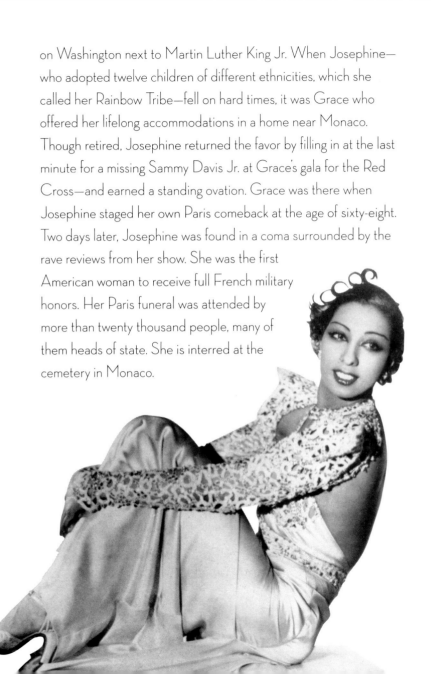

## TRAGEDY AND TRIUMPH

Unfortunately, it may have been tragedy that created the strongest bond between these two friends. Both desperate to have children, they would suffer several miscarriages before their children were born. Audrey had a very hard time carrying a baby to term, and retired to Switzerland in her final months. Sophia had it worse. In fact, to have a successful pregnancy, she had to spend all nine months in bed.

When one reporter inelegantly asked how having so many miscarriages felt, Sophia replied, "You feel bad about it, yes. Bad?! It becomes an obsession." She elaborated on her struggle in another interview. "If you want something very badly and know that with a great effort you can get what you want, then of course you make the effort," Sophia said. "If it's not all just words and sounds, but something you can actually do, then of course you do it. And if there had been just one chance in a million for me to have a child, I would have taken that one chance."

In the end, the joys of motherhood outweighed the agony of loss. Both were blessed with two sons. Audrey had Sean and Luca, Sophia had Carlo Jr. and Edoardo. "I guess I was born to be a mother, and if I could have had more than two sons, if I could have had daughters as well, and dozens of them, then I certainly would," Audrey said.

## LOVE LESSONS

Both Audrey and Sophia longed for the same thing from an early age—stability. And stability meant marriage and children. As devoted wives and mothers, they expected the same commitment from the men they held so dear.

When it came to their families, Audrey and Sophia found the idea of infidelity intolerable. "I have loved Carlo for my whole life, but I would leave him immediately if he were unfaithful to me," Sophia said. "Because I don't deserve infidelity. I don't believe that men can do anything they want and women cannot."

It was Audrey who would struggle with this problem the most. Even while she was pregnant with their son, her second husband, Andrea Dotti, kept turning up in the papers on the arm of one starlet or another. It was difficult and downright embarrassing. "Marriage should only be one thing," she said. "Two people decide they love each other so much that they want to stay together. Whether they sign a piece of paper or

*If you judge people, you have no time to love them.*

*Mother Teresa*

not, it's still a marriage, with a sacred contract of trust and respect. To me, the only reason to be married and stay married is just that. . . . So, if in some way I don't fulfill what he needs in a woman emotionally, physically, sexually, or whatever it is—and he feels he needs somebody else, then I could not stick around. I'm not the kind to stay and make scenes."

In the end, both women evolved their concept of what marriage really means. Though Sophia had struggled for years to legally marry Carlo, she would later say, "We are together because we like to be together, not because we have to be together. If it's a pleasure to be with someone, then your pleasure doesn't need papers or signatures: it's just your choice. And I think the pleasure is reciprocated."

After two divorces, Audrey found love with her companion Robert Wolders. When asked why they did not marry, her response was simple. "Why bother? It's lovely this way. The idea is, sort of, more romantic. Because it does mean we're together because we want to be. Not because we have to be. It's a slight difference, but maybe it's a very good one."

## WOMEN OF THE WORLD

Icons, actresses, wives and mothers, Audrey and Sophia chose to live as privately as possible. But when it came to a worthy cause, they both found that they could use their fame for good. UNICEF—an organization that often works in war-torn countries—provided the perfect platform.

Arguably their most devoted advocate, Audrey began working with UNICEF as a Goodwill Ambassador in 1988. When

faced with the devastating realities of trying to save the world's children, she said: "I go through my soul-searching. What can I do? What am I going to go and do there? But for all of us there's something we can do. It's true you can't take care of a thousand. But, finally, if you can save one, I'd be glad to do that."

Between the years 1988 and 1992, she would take up missions in Turkey, South America (Venezuela and Ecuador), Central America (Guatemala, Honduras and El Salvador), Sudan, Bangladesh and Vietnam. Her last visit, made in September 1992, and by far her hardest was to famine-stricken Somalia. "I want to be very careful how I say this," she said of her experience there. "I don't want to sound overly dramatic. But you really wonder whether God hasn't forgotten Somalia." During the time Audrey worked with UNICEF, the donation funding doubled.

No doubt inspired by her friend, Sophia was appointed as a Goodwill Ambassador for the United Nations High Commissioner for Refugees in Geneva in 1992. Just three months after Audrey had visited, Sophia also visited Somalia.

She was surely thinking of her friend Audrey's experience when she said, "When I come back maybe I'm going to be a different person, because whatever I see over there it's going to be something so incredible that it may change my whole life." After her visit, she echoed the heartbreak of witnessing an entire people on the brink of starvation. "It's a tragedy on a biblical scale," Sophia said. "The impact of children like skeletons, of disease, were so brutal. As soon as I closed my eyes last night these images came back and I had a terrible night."

Shortly after Audrey's last UNICEF trip to Somalia, she was diagnosed with cancer. She would live out her final few months surrounded by family and friends in Switzerland and would lose her battle in January of the following year, 1993.

On such a sad occasion, her dear friend Sophia said, "Audrey was meek, gentle and ethereal, understated in both her life and in her work. She walked among us with a light pace, as if she didn't want to be noticed. [I regret losing her] as a friend, as a role model and as a companion of my youthful dreams."

*Julie Andrews and Carol Burnett*

# Chapter Two

# FRIENDS SING EACH OTHER'S PRAISES

he first time I saw Julie Andrews close up she came into Whelan's drugstore at 44th Street and Broadway, the Sardi's of the unemployed actors, to buy a refill for her eyelash curler," Carol recalled. "Having stood through *My Fair Lady* four times, I rose as she entered out of force of habit— as though Queen Victoria had just appeared. I bought the same refill for my eyelash curler, only I never could get it in straight."

Two years would pass before Julie and Carol would meet. Though they were raised on different sides of the world, they shared many things in common, not the least of which was having survived alcoholic parents. They shared a passion for the stage and a wry, sometimes self-deprecating, sense of humor. One fateful night they were introduced in a Chinese restaurant and they took it from there—building a lifetime of song, laughter and love.

## CHOPSTICKS AND CHATTER

In the early sixties, both women were working in New York. Julie was performing in the Broadway run of *Camelot* while Carol was starring in the musical *Once Upon a Mattress*. "I had a manager called Lou Wilson and he knew Carol and he said, 'I think you two are going to get on like a house on fire,'" Julie remembered.

"We met at Ruby Foo's (Julie thinks that Chinese food, like the Statue of Liberty, is one of the glories of American civilization)," Carol remembered. "Over

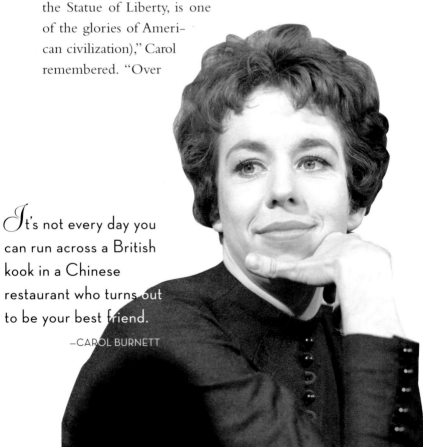

It's not every day you can run across a British kook in a Chinese restaurant who turns out to be your best friend.

—CAROL BURNETT

the egg-drop soup we traded anxieties: We're both devout cowards about airplanes and opening nights and criticism (the least little bit makes me contemplate slashing my wrists) and then we discussed our hair color (hers is natural—wouldn't you know).

"During the sweet-and-sour pork we compared our hideous childhoods: Julie swears she was buck-toothed and piano-legged and faintly wall-eyed for years: I was so tall the only thing that boys admired about me was my ability to outrun them, which was not what I had in mind.

"By the time the fortune cookies appeared," Carol recalled, "we were working out a plan to work together, some time somehow. The idea of teaming Miss Raggedy Ann Burnett, Girl Kook, with the remote, ladylike silver-throated Miss Andrews, 'ere from England to grace our humble U.S. shores, finally roused our poor escorts into calling for the check and stumbling out of the restaurant, holding their various heads."

*Each friend represents a world in us, a world possibly not born until they arrive, and it is only by this meeting that a new world is born.*

*Anaïs Nin*

## STAGE PRESENTS

They would first team up for a spot on *The Garry Moore Show*, where Carol was a regular. "I appeared with Carol for the first time on *The Garry Moore Show* for one simple reason: I needed the money. Also, they promised I wouldn't have to sing anything from *Fair Lady*," Julie said.

When Carol asked her what sort of number she would like to do, Julie said she had never played a cowboy. Carol, a native Texan, thought it was a great idea. Especially coming from a prim and proper Brit. "We did a song called 'Big D,' " Julie remembered, "which was all about Dallas. We did cowboy outfits with big hats. It was great fun, great fun." Carol was pretty good at the Texas drawl required, but it was Julie's British lilt turned Texan that gave the number a whole new twist.

It was good, but it was just a beginning. Julie and Carol wanted to do an hour-long special together, but bringing the duet to television would take some doing. "Everybody was excited about it except the networks," Carol recalled. "I wasn't yet under contract to CBS, and nobody had heard of Julie west of New Jersey. We went everywhere trying to sell the idea—to NBC, ABC and XYZ, but nobody was interested."

Ultimately, Carol convinced execs at CBS to do the show and "Julie and Carol at Carnegie Hall" was born. The show began with the catchy and cute "You're So London," and featured a rousing (and soon to be ironic) parody of Broadway's *The*

When we met it was just like instant friendship. It was just like heaven and we have been friends ever since.

—JULIE ANDREWS

*Sound of Music* with a reprise of "Big D" for the finale. Not only was the show a huge hit, it also earned two Emmys. "We had the time of our lives doing that show (maybe that's why it was a success) even though the rehearsals were so grueling we wondered whether we'd survive. We lived on tea and pep pills and developed psychosomatic colds," Carol remembered. It was so successful that just two months later, CBS signed Carol to a ten-year contract.

Julie had been performing since she was nine or so— in vaudeville, on stage and even once with the Queen of England in the audience—but there was something unusually special about performing with Carol. "Normally, when I work, I'm here and the audience is there," Julie said, "and I

hope to hell that they'll like me—but I stay terribly reserved just in case they don't. Carol knocks that out of me totally, and I'm able to clown around without destroying my defenses, because I know I have an ally up there with me. I'm not frightened by an audience when I'm performing with Carol; I'm hardly aware of the audience. It's some weird thing that happens—and I know that with me a much more real quality comes through. God knows, Carol doesn't need this; yet I must give her something back, because so often I feel that magic happens when we work together."

*We both started performing as kids. We both came from alcoholic families, we both had been caretakers, which is a tremendous burden for a kid. Being raised in a chaotic household, we were also both super-neat and super-square.*

*—JULIE ANDREWS*

"Working opposite her is like having Winston Churchill for your copilot. She never panics," Carol said. "Her *Fair Lady* director, the late Moss Hart, once said, 'She has that terrible English strength that makes you wonder why they lost India.' Among the cast she was known as The Rock, a reference to her sheer staying power."

# Girls Will Be Girls

In January 1965, Mike Nichols, Julie and Carol were summoned to Washington to perform at President Lyndon B. Johnson's inauguration. When Mike arrived, the ladies went out by the elevator to wait for him. "We sat on a settee across from the elevator and tried to think of something to make Michael laugh," Carol said. "We tried a lot of pigeon-toed stuff, then with our feet out, but nothing was funny enough. Julie said, 'I know what—Let's be kissing.' I said, 'I like you a whole lot, Julie, but I don't know.' She talked me into it, and went into a mad embrace the minute the elevator doors started to open. A woman got out. She didn't recognize us, but the look she gave us—Next time the doors opened we went into another mad embrace, and this time it was about ten male heads—none of them Mike's—who had stopped at the wrong floor. By now I'm on the floor in hysterics. Back comes the lady. She keeps looking and very solemnly said, 'You're Carol Burnett, aren't you?' I said, 'Yes, and that's Mary Poppins.' I wasn't gonna be the only one recognized. She goes, and the elevator opened again, and we go into our mad embrace. And damn Mike Nichols! He walks right out and by and says, 'Hi, girls,' like we did it all the time!"

# THAT HAPPY NUN

Not terribly long after their special aired, Walt Disney brought Julie the idea of starring as the mysterious and magical supernanny Mary Poppins. But Julie wasn't too sure she should. Carol remembered, "When the Poppins part came up she asked me, 'Do you think I ought to? Go work for Walt Disney? The cartoon person?' I assured her that Disney did other things besides cartoons, but she was a little worried about it. But when she came out to Hollywood she became totally enthusiastic. I don't think she ever came out here to be the great big star of the world, but she was very excited about that one movie."

Carol had helped to launch what would be one of Hollywood's most beloved screen actresses. In the next two years, Julie would go on to star in *The Americanization of Emily* and *The Sound of Music.* "We were always putting *The Sound of Music* down," said Carol, "and Julie always made fun of that happy nun. I'm not sure Richard Rodgers was awfully pleased when she was offered the movie. And I think he was concerned about her being Gwendolyn Goodie Two-Shoes. She sent me pictures from Austria of her in her nun's habit, which was a big laugh."

"I thought it might be awfully saccharine," Julie said. "After all, what can you do with nuns, seven children and Austria?" Of course, that happy nun would become Julie's most iconic role.

While Julie was making her mark on the big screen, Carol

"There are so many kinds of friendship: those from childhood and school; friendships—the passing friendships, the faraway ones; the I-would-do-anything-for-you, the understanding, compassionate; the part-time social and the work friendships. . . . For me, there is still nothing to compare with the sound of a *familiar voice filled with warmth and welcome* when I pick up the phone."

—LAUREN BACALL

*Carol probably brings out the worst in me. We bonded the minute we first met and usually do wicked, silly, naughty things whenever we get together.*

—JULIE ANDREWS

was defining a golden age in television. After a series of comedy and musical specials, *The Carol Burnett Show* debuted in September 1967, ran through 1978 and continues in syndication today. Winning twenty-four Emmys and eight Golden Globes in its eleven years, the weekly show assembled such stellar talents as Harvey Korman, Vicki Lawrence, Lyle Waggoner and Tim Conway, and included special celebrity guests. On the show, Carol perfected her now famous Tarzan yell and always ended the program with a tug to her ear, a message that said, "I love you, grandmother."

"In this carnivorous business we're in," Julie noted, "there's absolutely no jealousy, no upstaging, no competition between Carol and me—and I'm not sure why. I suppose it could be because neither of us sees the other as a threat; we each have our own area in which we do reasonably well, yet I think we feel stronger when we work together."

Julie and Carol would unite their talents once more in the 1971 special "Julie and Carol at Lincoln Center," which was nominated for three prime-time Emmys, and again in 1989 in "Julie and Carol: Together Again," also nominated for three Emmys and for which Carol won the American Comedy Award for Funniest Female Performer in a TV Special.

"When I am working with her, she is such a consummate comedienne that I feel that I have to pull myself up a notch or two to equal her and I really mean that most sincerely," Julie said. "She allows me a certain kind of freedom that I know I can cut up and be foolish and stupid and we are pretty idiotic with each other, I must say."

# Carole King and James Taylor

"Winter, spring, summer or fall, all you got to do is call, and I'll be there. Yes I will. You've got a friend." James was sitting in the balcony of the Troubadour in West Hollywood when he first heard these words performed by his friend singer/songwriter Carole. Although she was rehearsing it for her upcoming album, *Tapestry*, when James asked to record it, she obliged. It was "amazingly typical of [her] generosity," James later said. Perhaps the greatest friendship song of all time, "You've Got a Friend" became James's signature song and helped to define the singer/songwriter era of the 1970s. Debuting twice in the same year, 1971, the song appeared on *Tapestry*, Carole's most successful album, and on JT's album *Mud Slide Slim and the Blue Horizon*. James's version hit number one on the Billboard Hot 100 on July 31, 1971, and won a Grammy Award for each of them: Best Pop Vocal Performance, Male (James), and Song of the Year (Carole). The pair reunited in 2007 to celebrate the fiftieth anniversary of the legendary Troubadour club, where their friendship began. The highlight of the night? A duet of the song they both made famous.

# STAGE MOTHERS

Just after taping their first special, Julie thought she might just be pregnant. "Carol was the first person I told when I suspected I was pregnant," Julie remembers. "I confided to her that I'd just sent off a specimen and if the little mouse died, I'd know for sure. And she said: 'Send me a message, no matter where I am, when you find out.'

"It was several weeks after our show was televised that I got the word. I phoned CBS and was told Carol was rehearsing and couldn't come to the phone, so I asked the operator just to give her my message. Carol insisted that at one point all the loudspeakers at CBS announced: 'We have a message for Carol Burnett from Julie Andrews: The mouse is dead.'"

The day Emma was born in England, Carol received a cable:

SHE'S HERE, KNOWN OFFICIALLY AS EMMA STOP
START LEADING A GOOD CLEAN LIFE STOP YOU'RE
HER GODMOTHER ——MOTHER WALTON

In 1969, Julie married her second husband, director Blake Edwards. In addition to Emma, Julie now became a stepmother to Blake's two children. Yet three was not enough. Julie and Blake would also adopt two Vietnamese girls. "One of Julie's greatest acts of courage as a woman was to adopt

those orphan infants with Blake," Carol said. "She was so devoted to them you completely forgot she wasn't their natural mother . . . and she gave up years of her professional life to care for them."

Julie, not for a lack of offers, decided to stay home with the family. "I would have never believed that I'd be able to stop working the way I did. I agreed to do just enough to keep my ego reasonably high. I attended ballet class for a while, but found it took up too much time. The days were terribly busy, though I couldn't tell you what I did except get involved with some charities. Finally I got down to essentials: Blake and the children."

Carol also had a full house with three daughters of her own with her husband, Joe Hamilton, a TV producer. "Carol relates to her own children in the same warm, generous, outgoing way she relates to every human being I've ever seen her come in contact with," Julie said. "She has time for people, no matter how trivial or irritating their wants may be. I've never seen a chink in that attitude, and it definitely isn't a gimmick. That's just the way she is, and I guess I admire her all the more for it because I'm not capable of it myself."

*It is one of the blessings of
old friends that you can afford to
be stupid with them.*

Ralph Waldo Emerson

## CAROL ON JULIE

"Should you meet Julie, you must not be deceived by that grande dame facade. Underneath her Rule-Britannia face beats the spirit of a rampant lion cub," Carol said. "This is a quality that's hard to document because it's elusive, so you'll just have to take my word for it: Julie Andrews is not Queen Victoria; she's an irrepressible British kook.

"That dressed innocence masks a basic gutsiness, a directness, a for-realness that's very rare, especially in women. Julie . . . can't fake anything, including friendship. When she likes you she calls you ten times a day (my little sister keeps threatening to put in a private line for us), and if she doesn't she refuses to come to the phone, but nicely.

"She's shy with strangers, but once she accepts you—watch out. She's sweet, modest, kind to animals, completely wacky. She's a brilliant practical joker, a writer of naughty limericks, a superb mimic, a collector of shaggy-elephant stories, a devotee of the bongo drum and a lover of soda fountains.

"Her humor is direct, offbeat, and sometimes off-color. Some of her best lines are better not in print, but those pear-shaped British inflections make them sound like pure poetry. With that accent and those china-blue eyes she seems like an engaging child trying out some new words she picked up from her older brother. There is no one else quite like her."

# JULIE ON CAROL

"When we get together, it's rather like shucking off responsibilities and playing with one's best friend again. I get very bawdy when I'm around Carol (which is odd, since she's really something of a Puritan). She releases some inhibition in me. I'm not sure why.

"Few people really understand that Carol does practically everything with grace. Sometimes she tries to look and sound awkward and tell those outrageous stories about herself, but beneath the joking she's always a gracious lady.

"She constantly comes out with things that rock me because they are so funny, yet when I think about it, I've seldom heard her swear or use the sort of language that comes easily to me when I'm irritated or upset. She can be totally open on a show, wear what she wants, say what she likes, yet she's never an exhibitionist about it. And I've decided that it's simply because she's a lady with a very special kind of code that she never wears on her sleeve but which is always there.

"Carol hates phoniness of any kind. She won't tolerate canned laughter, for example, and she hates false notes in human relations just as passionately. Still, it's very rarely you see her expose emotion in

When Julie and I first started, we talked about men. Later on we talked about children. Then it was how do we keep in good shape? Now we talk Metamucil.

—CAROL BURNETT

52

"Throughout my professional life Estelle is the one I've turned to when shattered by the necessity of making a decision—a decision that may be freighted with weal or woe. She has never failed me. Fragile and delicate in appearance—as one critic observed, a snowflake would give her a concussion—Estelle is *granite* in a crisis. A world with more Winwoods would be a more desirable sphere on which to fret and fume."

—TALLULAH BANKHEAD
ON ESTELLE WINWOOD

any sad way. Usually it's a funny way—like the story she tells over and over about falling in love with her doctor and going to him for a shot and trying to act nonchalant when he told her it would have to be in the fanny. When he finished, she got up, walked straight into his closet instead of the corridor, and huddled there for 15 minutes, too humiliated to come out.

"I don't really know why, but the greatest danger in trying to describe Carol is always that she'll come through as a sort of one-dimensional Goody Two-Shoes, a modern Mary Poppins strewing goodness and light wherever she goes. Carol is so much more than that. She's complex and subtle and many-dimensional. She's wonderfully uninhibited, but she can also be a very private person. The surprises in her are hard to see and harder to describe to people who don't know her.

"The things I first liked about Carol haven't changed a bit," Julie noted. "She's ingenuous, she's straight, and she's real. What comforts me most in this dizzying world is that I know I can trust Carol completely. She's a sister to me and I love her a lot."

*Coco Chanel*
*and*
*Misia Sert*

# Chapter Three

# FRIENDS CHANGE THE WORLD

hey were an unusual pair—one a self-made woman consumed with work and the other a woman whose purpose, it seemed, was to inspire the great works of others. Misia Sert began as something of a mentor to Gabrielle "Coco" Chanel, making her the first fashion designer to be properly received into Parisian society. Yet Coco would eventually eclipse Misia in fame and influence as she built an empire that revolutionized women's fashion. Through various countries, lovers and quarrels, their complex friendship kept them side by side to the end.

# THE FRENCH CONNECTION

From the moment they met at the Parisian dinner party of a mutual acquaintance on May 28, 1917, Misia, a woman used to being in the know, was immediately taken by this new and mysterious stranger. "Despite the fact that she did not say a word, she radiated a charm I found irresistible. . . . Therefore I arranged to sit next to her after dinner," she said of Coco, ten years her junior. "During the exchange of banalities appropriate to a first meeting in a drawing room, I learned that she was called Mademoiselle Chanel and that she had a milliner's shop in Rue Cambon."

While Coco was just making a name for herself, Misia was already well known as a devoted friend and muse to some of the greatest artists of the time. Misia was born into her role as muse; early influences included her father, a painter/sculptor, and her grandfather, a virtuoso violinist who taught her notes before the alphabet. The composer Franz Liszt was a family friend. By the time she was a teenager, she was making her living by teaching piano lessons and was dreaming of one day taking the stage. It was these gifts, combined with an uncanny ability to make men fall in love with her, that helped her make her mark.

At the tender age of twenty-one, she married her first husband (and cousin), Thadée Natanson. He became the cofounder of the important *La Revue Blanche*, a review supported by such

*Life* as actually experienced is of little account. But the life one has dreamed of, that's what matters, because it will continue after one's death.

—COCO CHANEL

writers as Marcel Proust and Oscar Wilde. Posters promoting the new review were created by Thadée's friends—Toulouse-Lautrec, Édouard Vuillard and Pierre Bonnard—and often featured Misia herself. As their favorite model, she came to symbolize the success and influence of *La Revue Blanche*.

When Thadée continually faced financial ruin, a benefactor appeared in the form of French newspaper magnate Alfred Edwards. He would provide the needed funding with one condition: that Misia become his wife. Whether she was in love or just a pawn in a bigger game, Misia was soon divorced from Thadée and became a newly married, newly wealthy socialite. Yet her new stance in life did not prevent her from staying close with the artists she held dear. She would pose for Renoir, a portrait that now hangs in London's Tate Gallery. Ravel dedicated "Le Cygne" ("The Swan"), one of the songs in his *Histoires naturelles* cycle, and "La Valse" ("The Waltz") to her.

Unfortunately, Misia's marriage to Alfred was not to last. His affair with another woman soured their trust and they divorced. Though Misia moved from marriage to marriage, she stayed true to one thing—her desire to be close to the artistic world. By the time she met the soon to be famous Coco Chanel, Misia was with her third husband—the painter José Maria Sert. It was this pairing that allowed Misia to further assert her place as muse among some of the greatest artists, musicians and performers of her time—Mallarmé, Reverdy, Cocteau, Morand, Stravinsky, Picasso and Diaghilev, just to name a few.

Her effect on these great artists was unmistakable but frequently indefinable. Perhaps it was her beauty or her charm or her intelligence, but somehow she brought forth greatness by just "being." Even Coco had a hard time describing her talent to inspire and make the talents of the artistic elite shine. "Misia is to Paris what the goddess Kali is to the Hindu pantheon," Coco said, "the goddess of both destruction and creation. . . .

Certainly Misia does not create, but in some twilight areas she does the useful and beneficent work of a phosphorescent larva."

At the time of their first meeting, Chanel had made only a small name for herself in hats, outfitting some of the most proper women of the day. "She seemed to me gifted with infinite grace," Misia recalled, "and when, as we were saying good night, I admired her ravishing fur-trimmed, red velvet coat, she took it off at once and put it on my shoulders, saying with charming spontaneity that she would be only too happy to give it to me. Obviously I could not accept it. But her gesture had been so pretty that I found her completely bewitching and thought of nothing but her." Misia knew instantly that she and Coco were meant to be friends. "The next day I could hardly wait to go to see her in the rue Cambon. In her little boutique one found sweaters, hats, accessories of all kinds. When I arrived, two women were there talking about her, calling her 'Coco.' I don't know why the use of this name upset me so, but my heart sank: I had the impression that my idol was being smashed. Why trick out someone so exceptional with so vulgar a name?"

Still, the friendship blossomed instantly. Surely Coco was drawn to Misia's indefinable charm, free spirit and artistic escapades—much like everyone else. That same evening, Coco invited Misia and her husband, José, to join her at her home for dinner. It would be the first of many such gatherings. Though the men at the table would change over the years— Pablo Picasso, Jean Cocteau, Igor Stravinsky, Sergei Diaghilev, Salvador Dali and others—the two women would remain constant companions for more than thirty years.

*What do we live for, if it is not to make life less difficult for each other?*

George Eliot

# One Enchanted Evening

I still remember a delightful Christmas party in the Rue Cambon. Cocteau had brought The Six. The group of young composers, headed by Satie, was enjoying all the glory of the Boeuf sur le toit. Poulenc had just shed the uniform. Auric was in love with Irene Laght; Honegger and Milhaud, not yet a father, already had a reputation behind them; although Milhaud was not yet the Saint-Saens of his generation. The ravishing and refreshing Germaine Tailleferre, Jane Bathori, Ricardo Vines, Stravinsky, Morand, Segonzac, Sert, Misia, Godebski, the Philippe Berthelots; we were about thirty.... Satie was telling me about a ballet. Suddenly he stopped talking, for Misia with her brioche on her head, anxious, smelling some dark intrigue, was drawing her chair closer. Satie, his spectacles askew, screening his mouth and goatee with his hand, mumbled to me, "Here's the cat. Let's hide our birds."

–COCO CHANEL

## ESCAPE TO ITALY

The first man Coco was ever to love was Arthur "Boy" Capel. It was Boy who had allowed her to steal his clothes to rework the fabrics for her own fashion designs. It was Boy who had inspired her to make dresses out of jersey, a fabric usually reserved for undergarments. It was Boy, her greatest champion, who had helped her set up her business behind the Hotel Ritz. When he was killed in an automobile accident in 1919, Coco was devastated. Misia and her husband, José, had just the solution: Venice. A world unto itself, it was also far, far away from all things Boy.

Venice was much beloved by Misia. On her first visit there in 1897, she wrote, "Venice is not only more beautiful than I had imagined, but more so than I had thought possible. . . . At times, I shut my eyes, unable to bear such splendor, and, for the slightest thing, would cry out of sheer happiness." It was this wonder that Misia hoped to share with Coco in her time of need.

While there, Coco improved upon her education in the arts, with José as her able-bodied guide. He proved to be "an ideal traveling companion, always bright and cheerful, a guide with a prodigious and baroque erudition. . . . He explained everything to me, took pleasure in educating me, and found that I had a natural taste which he preferred to his knowledge."

In addition to art education, Venice provided the opportunity to meet new and interesting people. While typically "tradespeople"—as couturiers were known—were not welcome among the "society people," Misia set out to change all that on Coco's behalf. While in Italy, Coco began her ascent to the top of the social class. "I immediately gave a huge dinner party to introduce my new friend to the 'gratin' gathered there," Misia wrote. "I invited Princess de Poix, Count and Countess Volpi, the Prince of Greece, in short, the smartest people I could find! Thanks to her unaffected charm she had a great success, and after the Italian season it was out of the question, once she was back in Paris, that anyone would dream of not inviting her!

"Today, when couturiers are not only invited everywhere," Misia continued, "but are almost the only people to give lavish parties to which everyone rushes, it is difficult to imagine the vast privilege conferred on Mademoiselle Chanel toward the end of the war, when the doors of salons opened for her! It was certainly without precedent and the forerunner of a good many upheavals."

*The holy passion of friendship is of so sweet and steady and loyal and enduring a nature that it will last through a whole lifetime, if not asked to lend money.*

*Mark Twain*

# CIRCLE OF FRIENDS

Back in Paris, Coco's evening dinners resumed. Elaborate dinner parties and a mix of stellar talent would come to mark the association between Misia and Coco. These often lavish parties always included the best of French society and the most innovative artists and musicians. More than anything else, both women enjoyed indulging in interesting conversation.

"Paris in 1925 was a perpetual party," remembered composer Georges Auric. "And Coco Chanel was the living symbol of every luxury and every extravagance of the period. First of all, she was beautiful. More than beautiful—glorious, glorious with infinite charm. She was extremely sure of her own importance in fashions; she knew she was right and said so without modesty. But this did not bother us, for in fact she was right. She was never mistaken."

Playwright and *Vogue* columnist Henry Bernstein wrote, "We dined and danced twice at the home of our very famous and admirable and very dear Gabrielle Chanel, in the midst of the delicate and endless reflections of mirrors, sumptuous lacquers, and the white violence of legions of peonies—joyful, subtle, moving evenings that left hundreds envious (all those who could not be invited despite the dimensions of the beautiful salons of the Faubourg Saint-Honoré)—truly magnificent parties, in which the long gowns gave back to the tango all its thrilling graces."

Surely they were interesting dinner companions, though

they represented opposite sides of the same coin. To the great artists that surrounded them, Misia was adored for her effervescence, on-point opinions and striking beauty. In her sensibility, art would always be above fashion. Yet none could deny the influence of Coco—an artist in her own right—who changed fashion for the masses. Her influence on society was equal to theirs. And her fame and fortune became much greater. Both women were known to be generous, opinionated and passionate. Both could always be relied upon as a friend and became known as benefactors for their friends. For a time, Picasso kept a room in Coco's Paris apartment, as did Misia. And though he was already known as one of the great composers of his time, Stravinsky also found a home for his family and financial assistance due to the kindness of Coco.

> "All I need is room enough to lay a hat and a few *friends.*"

—DOROTHY PARKER

# THE FASHION REVOLUTION

Coco was perhaps best known for her timeless elegance. Her classic Chanel suits still remain in style. She was the first to produce the little black dress and an extensive line of costume jewelry (some of which was even designed by Misia herself). Yet she also rebelled against the conventions of the day, making and wearing clothes that allowed for more freedom and functionality. She had long ago embraced swimming and sunbathing—at the time, unheard-of pleasures—donning one of the first bathing suits made from the material of Boy Capel's sweaters. She had worn a ponytail. She would go on to produce beach pajamas—pants for women, a scandal!

Perhaps none had greater admiration for the talent and influence of Coco than her friend Misia. She wrote, "It was just after the war that Mademoiselle Chanel, whose establishment in the rue Cambon was rapidly expanding to dizzying heights, transformed women at one stroke by eliminating their corsets, their whalebone stays, their chokers—and even their hair. Gone were the flashy frills and furbelows—vanished miraculously along with the cinched petticoats and the bodices laced to the point of suffocation. Women's bodies took a new shape; bosoms and bottoms disappeared—while legs suddenly appeared where formerly one had only glimpsed a chaste ankle. . . . "

Often her choice to defy convention came along by necessity. For example, on one trip to Venice, Coco made a remarkable discovery. "One day on the Lido, tired of walking on the hot sand barefoot and burning my feet with leather sandals, I had a boot maker from Zattere cut a sheet of cork in the form of a sole and added some thongs," Coco remembered. "Ten years later, the windows at Abercrombie's in New York were full of shoes with cork soles."

Of all her inventions and re-inventions, Coco would rather immodestly say, "I invented sportswear for myself. I set the fashion for the very reason that I was the first twentieth-century woman."

# SCENT OF A WOMAN

One day, a friend came for a visit with Misia, bringing with him a manuscript—*The Secret of the Medicis*—containing a recipe that purportedly made it possible for empresses and queens to stave off the curses of old age and maintain a youthful vitality. Created by René the Florentine, the potion, Misia's friend claimed, "guarantees permanent, indestructible youth." Immediately, Misia had a big idea to share with her friend Coco.

"Ten minutes later I was sitting opposite Coco and busily explaining, with all the glib poise of a first-class traveling salesman, the marvelous success she could have by creating a Chanel toilet water based on the unbelievable *Secret of the Medicis*," Misia wrote. "Her name was then on everyone's lips and in itself a guarantee of success.

"A few weeks later, *L'Eau de Chanel* made its appearance. It succeeded far beyond our wildest hopes. It was unbelievable, almost as if we had won first prize in the lottery! 'Why don't you really go in for perfumes?' I said to Coco. 'It seems to me, after the success of *L'Eau de Chanel*, that René the Florentine is the goose that laid the golden egg.'

"At that moment, Mademoiselle Chanel, who at first considered the toilet water a plaything, had the genius to see the future possibilities of this new idea. And from the start, her perfumes were so successful that Chanel Number 5, Number

22 and *Bois des Îles* were soon in demand on all five continents."

While some say that Coco thought five her lucky number, it was in fact the fifth concocted scent presented to her by perfumer Ernest Beaux. Though, given its success, one might dare to believe that five was Coco's lucky number indeed.

Chanel's perfumes created a new line of goods not tried before—her most successful business venture—and it was not long before the other fashion houses followed suit.

*A Friend may well be reckoned the masterpiece of Nature.*

Ralph Waldo Emerson

"It's often just enough to be with someone. I don't need to touch them. Not even talk. A *feeling* passes between you both. You're not alone."

—MARILYN MONROE

## LA MODE AMERICAINE

"I have been asked a hundred times by Americans to go to California to create fashions. I refused, knowing that the solution would be artificial, and so negative," Coco once said. Only Sam Goldwyn was able to persuade her to give it a try. He wanted his stars Chanel-clad both on- and offscreen, and he was prepared to pay her one million dollars to come to Hollywood twice a year with her designs. With America in the midst of a depression, Goldwyn felt that the French fashions would only heighten the appeal of his movies to the public.

In 1931, Coco left Paris for California, with Misia by her side. Sert, Misia's husband, had recently left her for a younger woman (whom Misia had trusted as a friend) and while Coco and Misia had already traveled together to England and Misia's beloved Italy, America offered all the glitz and glamour to ease her thoughts away from her loss.

On their arrival, the women were met by the likes of Greta Garbo, Marlene Dietrich and Gloria Swanson. Coco's first assignment was to design the clothes for an Eddie Cantor musical comedy called *Palmy Days*. While filming was happening at a breakneck pace, Chanel did manage to design a few dresses for the film's leading lady, Charlotte Greenwood. It wasn't long before she and Misia headed back to Paris, but what she saw while in Hollywood stayed with her. She was appalled that the studio system seemed to rob women of their identities and turn them into paid servants at the whim of their producers.

Her next assignment was to design the clothes for reigning box office queen Gloria Swanson's next film *Tonight or Never*. The task was not an easy one. Miss Swanson was pregnant, and she didn't want anyone to know. Not even Chanel. The fittings were scheduled in Paris so that Chanel could stay at her shop at Rue Cambon. But at each fitting the clothes became tighter. A girdle was out of the question, since it showed beneath the sheer fabric. "Lose five pounds!" was Chanel's response. This

*I don't like people talking about the Chanel fashion. Chanel—above all else—is a style. Fashion, you see, goes out of fashion. Style never.*

—COCO CHANEL

was, of course, not possible. Instead Swanson asked Chanel to produced a rubberized undergarment that would eliminate lines and keep her thin enough through the picture. Chanel was not happy. After all, she had worked hard to eliminate the corset from women's fashion. Yet with the usual Chanel creativity, the clothes were produced to make the pregnancy less visible, including a bias-cut evening gown in black satin and a suit that was also in a signature Chanel style.

The successful completion of the job should have cemented Chanel's role as a Hollywood costumer. And while many of the day's top actresses were anxious to work with her, others refused her service. For Chanel, trying to clothe stars who had opinions nearly as strong as hers, for a studio system that left her disgruntled, proved too much. She refused to produce anything but her own brand of elegance, and that was best done at her showroom, where she had complete control. Sam Goldwyn, thankfully, never did ask for his money back.

## LA VIE DE L'AMOUR

Notoriously unlucky in love, though not without suitors, Coco had a long succession of unusually interesting lovers—Arthur "Boy" Capel, French poet Pierre Reverdy, the Russian Grand Duke Dmitri Pavlovich, the wealthy English duke of Westminster and French artist Paul Iribe (born Iribarnegaray) among them. And it was Misia who knew all their secrets.

Coco had been asked to marry on several occasions, yet she always refused. And then she met Iribe. He was a renowned fashion illustrator and designer, and she felt she had finally met the man of her life. Surprisingly willing to forgo her freedom in favor of love, she got engaged. For three years, they inspired each other, shared their lives and inevitably made plans for the future. Until the summer of 1935, when Iribe collapsed with a heart attack during a game of tennis as Coco watched helplessly. At the age of fifty-two she was once again heartbroken and alone.

Misia did her best to comfort her, as they had always done for each other, but to no avail. Coco returned to Paris and once more immersed herself in work. "All her life, at bottom she had been looking for happiness," remarked her confidant Serge Lifar, "and she never really found it. So she took her revenge with fame and success. She was never very happy in love, though she looked for it everywhere. . . . But starting with a certain dose of egocentricity is a handicap for loving and being loved. That was Chanel's drama."

# Dorothy Parker and Robert Benchley

The fated meeting happened at *Vanity Fair*—she was the drama critic and he the managing editor. When the higher-ups were away in Europe, they began taking languorous spirit-filled lunches at the Algonquin Hotel, and the Algonquin Roundtable (also called the Vicious Circle) was born. Though they were the closest of friends and collaborators, Robert always called Dorothy Mrs. Parker. When Dorothy was fired from *Vanity Fair* for what the staff considered an unfair

reason, Robert quit out of solidarity, despite the fact that he had a wife and two children to support. Dorothy said, "It was the greatest act of friendship I'd ever seen." They went on to create a freelance writing partnership, which they named Park-Bench. Their office was less than lavish. "One cubic foot less of space and it would have constituted adultery," Robert said.

# ADIEU

Throughout their lives, Coco and Misia shared many things: friends, homes, success and fame. Along the way, Misia helped Coco as interior decorator, jewelry designer and confidant. Both of them strong and self-assured, they were best friends who encouraged, consoled and delighted each other.

Coco confessed that Misia had been her only female friend. And with tongue in cheek, she said, "We like others only for their faults, and Misia has given me ample and numerous reasons to like her. Misia sticks by only what she does not understand; meanwhile she understands almost everything. I have remained a mystery to her, which explains a loyalty that, while always crazy, recovers—after certain lapses—its constancy."

Ironically, for all the arts and culture that swarmed around her, for all the artists on whom she had influence, Misia was not always a woman of cultured ways. Yes, she played the piano beautifully, was well known as a charmer and had a fascination with bejeweled miniature trees, but Misia was not particularly interested in pursuits beyond the artists she loved. "Misia— from the time she was fifteen years old, ever since Valvins, where with hair and sleeves rolled up she posed the brothel girls for Toulouse-Lautrec, Renoir, Vuillard and Bonnard, all the way to Picasso, Stravinsky, and Diaghilev—has lived fifty years among the greatest artists, and yet . . . she has never opened a book," Coco said. "She does not even read her mail!" Of course, who but your closest friend could make such an observation and get away with it.

When Misia passed away at the age of seventy-eight, it was Coco who closed off her bedroom and took on the work of getting the body ready for presentation. Just as she had in life, Coco stood beside her dear friend in death, making sure that she looked her best.

"I just would like to show the important role that such a woman played in our time," Misia wrote about Coco. "I felt it so strongly that, from our first meeting, I could hardly wait to make others aware of it. One could say that it is easy to help a beautiful diamond to shine. Still, it was my privilege to help it emerge from its rough state, and—in my heart—to be the first person dazzled by its brilliance."

*Lucille Ball*
*and*
*Vivian Vance*

# Chapter Four

# FRIENDS BECOME FAMILY

*B*efore *Friends*, before *Sex and the City*, there were Lucy and Ethel. An inseparable pair, there was no end to the number of predicaments they would get into—and out of—together, keeping us laughing all along the way. Playing neighbors and best friends, they made television history.

*I Love Lucy* debuted on October 15, 1951. Within three weeks of going on the air, it was the number one show on television. Together, Lucy and Vivian would help define the new medium. While it wasn't always smooth sailing behind the scenes, what began as on-screen chemistry evolved into a friendship that withstood grueling schedules, failed marriages, fame and more than its fair share of funny moments.

## FIRST IMPRESSIONS

When they were first introduced on set, Lucy's response was, "She doesn't look like a landlady."

"I can look different," Vivian promised.

When Lucy went on to say that Ethel had to be dumpy, Vivian said, "I photograph dumpy."

It was not exactly love at first sight.

Lucy was known for throwing her weight around, having tantrums and most often saying exactly what was on her mind. She was not always easy to live with.

"My mother had a way of testing people," remembered her daughter, Lucie Arnaz. "If you were the kind of person who gave it right back to her, she wouldn't do it to you. But if you let her walk on you, she would do it continually. She got off on that power of being able to tell you what to do. The few peo-

ple in her life who said, 'Excuse me, I'm a human being,' in a nice way, especially if they had a sense of humor, then she had enormous respect for those people."

Not far into the first season, Vivian was asked how she could go on living with Lucy's bad behavior. She reportedly told a friend, "Honey, listen, if this show should be a hit, it could be the biggest thing that ever happened to my career. So, I made up my mind, I'm going to learn to love that bitch!"

After a while, Vivian learned just how to handle Lucy's outbursts. She would simply say, "Okay, honey, you own the store. It's all right with me." At which Lucille would always fall apart laughing, which was the way to her heart. It would not be long before Vivian was an empowered opinion on and off the set.

*I no doubt deserved my enemies, but I don't believe I deserved my friends.*

Walt Whitman

# BEING ETHEL

Everyone should have a best friend like Ethel Mertz. Making her entrances with a cheery, "Hi, honey," Vivian was often referred to as "TV's most beloved second banana." She served as confidant, companion and foil. Yet the real-life Vivian was a far cry from the frumpy Ethel we came to know and love on screen.

Before she met Lucy, Vivian had a blossoming stage career. The New York critics noted that she was the embodiment of a "hussy," "blonde menace," and "alluring vixen." Ethel Mertz? Really?

Desi first saw her in a one-week stint in *The Voice of the Turtle* at the famed La Jolla Playhouse. He hired her on the spot. But Vivian was reluctant. "Nobody in their senses would choose to go into television. In 1951, it was a silly new third entity that attracted little attention. . . . Television? Not for me, thank you. . . . Take on a full-time job in a medium that didn't amount to anything? The strain involved wasn't worth it. Besides, what could it lead to? No series anything like this *I Love Lucy* had been successful so far.

"But Desi kept phoning. Finally, against my better judgment, I agreed to take the job for thirteen weeks at $350 a week. Desi couldn't promise that the show would continue beyond that." Not only did it continue, it made television history.

Still, Vivian would never get comfortable with the dowdiness of Ethel Mertz. "Up until then, she'd usually been cast in glamorous 'other woman' parts," Lucy said. "But she went along gamely with Ethel Mertz's dowdy clothes, no false eyelashes or eye makeup, and hair that looked as if she had washed and set it herself. But she drew the line at padding her body to look fatter."

Legend has it that a clause in her television contract required Vivian to stay twenty pounds heavier than Lucy. Actually, the

If I walked down Fifth Avenue alone, people would recognize me and watch me go. If Lucy walked down Fifth Avenue alone, people would recognize her but not come up to her, and just let her go. But if the two of us walked down Fifth Avenue, we'd stop traffic.

—VIVIAN VANCE

only contract like this was a gag gift from Lucy. Vivian did, however, dye her hair and wear housedresses that were a few sizes smaller to make her appear overweight.

"On summer vacations, she'd diet, and once she came back on the set positively svelte," Lucy recalled. " 'Well, Vivian,' I kidded her, 'you've got just two weeks to get fat and sloppy again.' "

Time and again Vivian told producer Jess Oppenheimer, "If my husband in this series makes fun of my weight and I'm actually fat, then the audience won't laugh . . . they'll feel sorry for me. But if he calls me a fat old bag and I'm not too heavy, then it will seem funny."

# BEING LUCY

Beginning as a model, by the late 1930s Lucy was known around the RKO lot as the "Queen of the B's." Her credits included roles with both the Three Stooges and the Marx Brothers. Around this time, a fortune-teller told her that one day she would be the richest woman and the biggest star in Hollywood.

When she met Desi Arnaz, she said, "It wasn't love at first sight. It took five minutes." Soon after, they eloped, garnering a lot of press attention. But when their careers kept them apart too often, they decided to find a way to work together. Soon enough they formed Desilu Productions and *I Love Lucy* was on its way.

"I never found a place of my own," Lucy said, "never became truly confident until, in the Lucy character, I began to create something that was truly mine. The potential was there. Lucy released it."

While her on-screen persona was often flighty and always well-meaning, the real-life Lucy was a force to be reckoned with. One of the greatest comic actresses of all time, she proved that women could be the lead and carry a show. Not one show, but several.

Her success was largely based on her drive and determination to get it right every time. In Vivian, she found a kindred spirit to rely on. "Vivian, like me, was a perfectionist who took her profession very seriously," Lucy said. " 'Now what's my motivation here?' she'd ask me or Desi or Jess, and this would launch into a half-hour discussion.

"I could sense a flaw in the story line or dialogue but I couldn't always put my objections into words," Lucy recalled. "Frustrated, Desi would burst into a flood of Spanish. I'd express my frustrations by getting mad. Vivian was a tower of strength in such circumstances; she would intuitively guess what was wrong and then analyze it. She would make a great director."

Lucy started her career at RKO at a rate of just seventy-five dollars a week.

Years later, in 1957, Desilu Productions would buy RKO for six million dollars cash. With thirty-three soundstages—four more than Metro-Goldwyn-Mayer and eleven more than Twentieth Century-Fox—Desilu became the largest filming empire in Hollywood. After her split from Desi, Lucy became the first female head of a Hollywood studio and one of the most powerful people in Hollywood. While running Desilu, her willingness to take a risk resulted in blockbuster TV series such as *Mission: Impossible* and *Star Trek*.

# A Royal Affair

One Sunday afternoon, Viv came over and we were doing our hair. We used to play "beauty parlor" like two idiots. We were like two teenagers, we'd have a couple of drinks and play games … you know, the usual stuff. Suddenly, there was a knock at the door. Since it was Sunday, the staff was off, and Desi was fishing in Del Mar, and Vivian and I were all by ourselves. I didn't want to answer the door, but they kept knocking and knocking, and I went to the window and twelve limousines were lined up and motorcycles and police cars with flashing lights, and Viv and I are dripping wet. I opened the door and people came running in, led by the Beverly Hills Chamber of Commerce. It was the nawab of Brunei or the sheik of Araby or the sultan of Swat. I didn't know who the hell he was except he was a head of state and all he wanted to do was to see where Lucy and Ricky lived. Here's Vivian and me with towels on our heads and people are running around taking pictures. The man from the chamber of commerce was very apologetic and said that it was an unscheduled stop. That's an understatement! The king

looked all around the lanai, the den, the kitchen, and then he looked at me and asked where Lucy was. I told him she was gone for the day, but I would be sure to tell her that he had stopped by. The entourage bowed their way out the door, and I slammed it behind them. Vivian was rolling on the floor holding herself. She couldn't stop laughing. The king hadn't recognized either of us. She said that we should use the incident in an episode for the show, but I said that I didn't think anyone would believe it.

—LUCILLE BALL

# MISERY NEEDS COMPANY

When *I Love Lucy* began, the already twice divorced Vivian was married to actor Phil Ober. Though he would guest star in two episodes of *I Love Lucy*, he didn't have many fans among the cast and crew.

"He was a terrible man," Lucy said. "Loved to embarrass her. He was nuts and he made her nuts. She was seeing all these shrinks. God, it was a mess. I told her to get rid of the guy, but if Vivian was one thing, it was loyal."

"My husband liked to dominate and discipline me," Vivian said. "I kept trying to please him, but nothing I did was right. There were times when I would literally beat my head against the bedroom wall in frustration."

"One day Viv came to work with a shiner," Lucy remembered. "That did it. I think I said to her, 'If you don't divorce him, I will.' And she did."

Around the same time, after close to twenty years of marriage, Lucy and Desi had finally decided to call it quits. She had once filed for divorce in 1944, but reconsidered. "During this period, Vivian Vance was getting her divorce from Phil Ober," Lucy recalled, "and she was upset and miserable too. Vivian and I have always been extraordinarily compatible, so we were especially close during this time of misery."

The breakup of Lucy and Desi was painful for the entire cast of *I Love Lucy*. After all, they had formed a family. "Those were emotional days for everyone on the show," Vivian remembered. "I still get misty-eyed when I talk about Lucy's and Desi's breakup. After their last show together, a lot of us just stood there and cried. The reason we were all so involved with the split was because we all shared a bond—the cast and crew were straight out of *Our Town*. We had a tight little circle and knew about all the fortunes and misfortunes of everyone's lives. It was like living in a small town and sharing every emotion."

"After Desi and I went into the final clinch and the lights dimmed, there were no laughs, no smiles," Lucy said. "The marriage, after nineteen years, had also ended that day. There is something about an ending—even when it is something you have wanted to end—that hurts inside.

"I hate failure and that divorce was a Number One failure in my eyes," noted Lucy. "It was the worst period of my life. Neither Desi nor I have been the same since, physically or mentally."

# SECOND ACTS

In January 1962, Lucy went east to try to persuade Vivian to team up with her again for *The Lucy Show*, a follow-up to the success of *I Love Lucy*. "I refused to even consider being in a continuing series without Vivian," remembered Lucy. "Since we had gone off the air, she had married a handsome and successful New York literary agent, John Dodds. They had bought a century-old house in Stamford, Connecticut, and Vivian was ecstatic about her flower garden, singing in the local church choir, and lecturing on behalf of mental health."

Vivian was hard to convince. "I don't want anything to happen to my marriage," Vivian said at the time. "All this flying back and forth is difficult. It's no fun working here. I get up, go to the studio, go home and fall into bed. It's lonely. If I were Lucy, I'd do what she's doing, but I don't want to own a studio.

I just own a beautiful farmhouse and yard filled with flowers that need attention, and I'd like to be there."

Vivian would finally agree to reunite with Lucy again, but it would take some doing. "Her loyalty to me—and a hefty paycheck—won her back to my side," Lucy said.

Tired of being known as the frumpy Ethel Mertz, Vivian asked to be more

*Lucy came east with a script in her purse for a new series for me. I said, "Lucy, don't take it out. I won't read it." And she didn't. And I didn't.*

—VIVIAN VANCE

glamorous—especially when it came to the clothes. And, just like Lucy, she wanted her name on the show to be her real name—Vivian. "Before the contract was signed, I had a talk with Desi," recalled Vivian. "'I'll come back,' I said, 'but I want a clause that says my name will be Vivian.' 'Okay, Veev, I understand.' He had run up against a similar problem as mine with Ethel. For nine years, he'd been Ricky Ricardo and lost his own identity." Vivian Bagley became the first divorcée ever portrayed on a weekly American television series.

"Vivian has always been the greatest supporting player anyone could ask for," Lucy said. "During one of the shows in this new series, we were supposed to be trapped in a glass shower stall, with the water turned on full blast. The script called for me to dive down and pull out the plug at the bottom of the shower, but when I did this in front of a live audience, I found I had no room to maneuver. I couldn't get back to the surface again. What's more, I had swallowed a lot of water, and was actually drowning, right there in front of three hundred people who were splitting their sides laughing.

"Vivian, realizing in cold terror what had happened, never changed expression. She reached down, pulled me safely to the surface by the roots of my hair, and then calmly spoke both sides of our dialogue, putting my lines in the form of questions. Whatta girl! Whatta night!"

"Friendship is very, very important. We take it for granted, and we have one life. If you've got a friend, enjoy it. Don't wait until someone passes on. Enjoy it while it exists, because it's rare. ... It's that kind of *blind loyalty and love* that makes a real friendship, and we had that real friendship."

—JACK KLUGMAN
ON HIS FIFTY-YEAR FRIENDSHIP
WITH COSTAR TONY RANDALL

# MAKING UP

"They'd been together so long, it was like Leopold and Loeb," remembered Carole Cook, Lucy's acting protégée and a member of the Desilu Workshop. "They had been through so much together. She trusted Viv. Viv was really the only one who would say, 'You know, honey, if you do things this way, you might get a bigger laugh.' They were always trying to help each other bring out something extra."

"As far as I was concerned, it was Kismet," Lucy remembered fondly. "Viv and I were extraordinarily compatible. We both believe whole-heartedly in what we call 'an enchanted sense of play,' and use it liberally in our show. It's a happy frame of mind, the light touch, skipping into things instead of plodding. It's looking at things from a child's point of view and believing. The only way I can play a funny scene is to believe it."

The relationship was not without its fights. Both Lucy and Vivian were strong women. Both knew what to do to get under the other's skin. But it was only rarely that the fights lasted beyond a few minutes. "One day Vivian and I had a disagreement on the set and stopped speaking," Lucy remembered. "The silence went on much longer than either of us anticipated. It got to be a nuisance, since we were so used to listening carefully to each other's lines and making suggestions. But this particular Thursday was spent in stony silence.

We fought like sisters and made up the same way.

—VIVIAN VANCE

108

"Finally, it was an hour before the actual performance. We usually spent this time buoying each other up to get into the proper relaxed and joyous mood for performing. We sat side by side, putting on our makeup. Although not a word had been spoken, I suddenly blurted out, 'Vivian, you know that line'— I repeated it—'you're not reading it right. It should be . . . ' And I gave her my interpretation.

" 'Gee,' she replied, 'you're right. Why didn't you say so before?'

" 'Well,' I replied heatedly, 'we weren't speaking, and I'd be damned if I'd tell you!'

"Our eyes met in the mirror and we collapsed into laughter. We could never stay cross with each other for very long."

# OFF AIR

By the third season of *The Lucy Show*, Vivian was ready to just be home. "I want to live at home with my husband," Vivian told the press. "I'm tired of commuting." Lucy very much wanted Vivian to stay on, offering not only more money but also the opportunity to produce, write and direct, territories rarely explored by women in the business. When Vivian asked for an astronomical fee, Lucy had to put business first and let Vivian go.

During the third season, Vivian was slowly written out of the series, though she would occasionally return for guest appearances. For the first time, the public had to get used to Lucy without her sidekick, Ethel.

Lucy would go on to do four more seasons of *The Lucy Show*. From 1968 to 1974, Lucy would star in *Here's Lucy*, with her son and daughter—Lucie and Desi—as her costars.

When she wrapped her final show of the *Here's Lucy* series, the real-life Lucy was none too sure what to do with herself. "It was one of the most traumatic events of my life," Lucy remembered. "It was a terrible thing for me—the loss of my creative arena. I lost not only the pleasure of being with my friends every day on the set, but also my identity. Being Lucy gave me a built-in intimacy with the public. I loved being her. I loved the antics and the gags. I enjoyed my work."

Vivian looked at her television career differently. "I don't think TV kept me from anything—my ambition was never to be a big star," she said. "I've seen very few happy stars, and I was determined that that wasn't going to happen to me. The plums hang so high and the vampires beckon, and I knew that if I fell for it, I'd be as unhappy as the other ladies in Hollywood. Ambition doesn't go well with age or companionship."

*The real marriage of true minds is for any two people to possess a sense of humour or irony pitched in exactly the same key, so that their joint glances at any subject cross like interarching searchlights.*

*Edith Wharton*

# Marlon Brando and Wally Cox

Marlon and Wally were nine years old when they met in Chicago. The boys became fast, albeit unlikely, friends. One would become the handsome, eccentric leading man, the other a witty, sometimes awkward comedian. It was a bond that would last for the rest of their lives. Early in their careers, they were roommates. (Cox reportedly moved out because he hated Marlon's pet raccoon.) And though their statures were very different, they relished all things athletic—swimming, motorcycles, hiking and wrestling. Both shied away from the press, preferring more intellectual conversations on unusual subjects. And Wally always knew just how to make

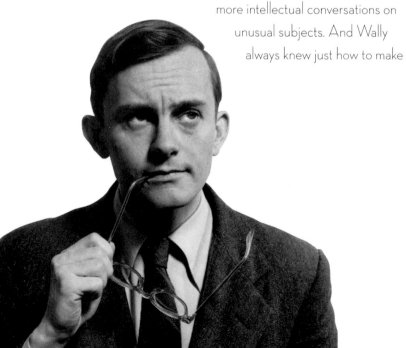

Marlon laugh. When Wally passed away in 1973, Marlon was asked to pick up his ashes at the mortuary on the agreement that he would scatter them in Death Valley where Wally loved to rock hunt and hike. Instead, Marlon kept the ashes in his house, sometimes transporting them in the front seat of his car, much to the dismay of his family. "I talk to him all the time," he said. Upon Marlon's death, the Brando family scattered the ashes of both men, together, in Death Valley.

# A LAST HURRAH

Their final collaboration came in 1977 with the special "Lucy Calls the President." Vivian had suffered a slight stroke and was left partially paralyzed. As a result, she was shot only at angles where the paralysis was not noticeable.

Though the special was not a huge success, it would prove to be the last on-screen appearance of two of the world's favorite television best friends—Lucy and Vivian. Just two years later, Vivian succumbed to bone cancer at the age of sixty-seven.

Desi spoke for both himself and Lucy when he said, "It's bad enough to lose one of the great artists we had the honor and the pleasure to work with, but it's even harder to reconcile the loss of one of your best friends."

"When she would talk of Vivian Vance and their relationship," noted Ann Dusenberry, her *Life with Lucy* costar, "her eyes would well up. She loved her and missed her desperately. After Viv was gone, I got the feeling that she was always seeking that kind of connection again. I just think Lucy wanted a friend."

During a 1986 interview, Lucille Ball talked about watching *I Love Lucy* reruns and her reaction to Vivian's performance: "I find that now I usually spend my time looking at Viv. Viv was sensational. And back then, there were things I had to do—I was in the projection room for some reason, and I just couldn't concentrate on it. But now I can. And I enjoy every move that Viv made. She was something."

"Isn't it wonderful that you see sisters sticking together? A lot of times when women reach a certain status, they don't have girlfriends on their same level. These are girls that I've been friends with for almost 20 years— Tisha [Campbell-Martin], Star [Jones]. We've been with each other through the good, bad and the ugly. The highs and the lows, the rollercoaster rides of success in the entertainment industry. The fact that we've made it through all that is the true *testament of sisterhood.*"

—VIVICA A. FOX

*Debbie Reynolds*
*and*
*Carrie Fisher*

# Chapter Five

# FRIENDS CAN
# SURVIVE ANYTHING

While some say you can't fight destiny—you will turn into your mother—it is true for Carrie Fisher more than most. "I've done exactly what my mother has done. I mean to a tee. My mother . . . did her first film at seventeen. Me too. Became famous at nineteen. Me too. Married a short Jewish singer. Me too. My last husband was four years younger and from the south. My mother's last husband—four years younger and from the south."

From the beginning, Debbie and Carrie have faced many challenges by each other's side—divorce, fame, drug addiction, illness and heartbreak. Nowadays they even share a driveway.

"I would say I have the mother who's perfect for me," Carrie said. "She's eccentric—oh, is she eccentric! And life has happened to her in a big way. I love her sense of humor; her work ethic; her being a real mother, a good mother—caring, loyal, and principled. She's also a really good friend."

## AMERICA'S SWEETHEARTS

Carrie (and her brother, Todd) are the products of one of the most famous couplings in Hollywood history. Dubbed "America's Sweethearts," Debbie and Eddie Fisher were often touted as the perfect American couple with the perfect American family.

Debbie won a beauty contest at just sixteen and left a very normal Texas childhood to begin her film career at MGM. The quintessential girl next door, she brought her wholesome, perky persona to the big screen. Her big break came in 1952 when she was teamed up with Gene Kelly in *Singin' in the Rain*. She was not yet twenty and not yet a dancer.

When she married Eddie Fisher in 1955, he was a red-hot star transitioning from teen idol to television. One of the most popular crooners of the 1950s, he had had seventeen songs in the Top 10 between 1950 and 1956 and he was two years into hosting his NBC television variety show, *Coke Time with Eddie Fisher*. From the outside looking in, they had it all—talent, fame, fortune and family.

While Debbie reigned supreme as one of the top ten box office stars of the year, life on the home front took a very unexpected turn. Two of their closest friends were Elizabeth Taylor and producer Mike Todd. When they married in Acapulco, Mexico, Eddie was the best man and Debbie the maid of honor. Tragically, just over a year later, Mike was killed in his plane, the *Lucky Liz*, near Grants, New Mexico. It wasn't long before Eddie asked Debbie for a divorce so he could marry Elizabeth. The press had a field day—think Jennifer, Brad and Angelina. Carrie was just eighteen months old.

Suddenly, Debbie was a single, working mother with two

*I* was angry losing my husband but Elizabeth and I have talked it through over the years. I think the main question we keep asking ourselves each time is this: how could we both have fallen for such a simpleton as Eddie Fisher?

—DEBBIE REYNOLDS

children to raise. While her name was splashed all over the gossip pages, she needed to provide for her family. "Well, you know, I've gone through a lot of different things in my life," she said. "A lot of attention-getting scandal and really difficult times with a huge amount of press coverage. They were on my front yard and in my backyard rooting through trees and looking in my windows. It was an awful experience."

Still, the best was yet to come. In 1964, Debbie was nominated for an Oscar as the lead in *The Unsinkable Molly Brown*, a role that would come to define her life. She was a survivor and she would forever be remembered as one.

# TEENAGE YEARS

At age thirteen, Carrie began touring with her mother's musical revue, and when Debbie opened in *Irene* on Broadway in 1973, Carrie sang in the chorus. By the time Carrie was seventeen, they were headlining at the Palladium in London. The reviewers said, "Debbie Reynolds is the gold of vaudeville, and she has brought us the platinum."

While they were in England, Carrie also auditioned for London's Central School of Speech and Drama and she got a scholarship. The only problem was, she didn't want to go. The disagreement drove a wedge between mother and daughter. "I went to war with my mother," Carrie said. "I rolled my eyes at most things she said. Who was she to tell me how to behave? Didn't she see that I was almost grown up and not in need of her antiquated, suspect counsel? Apparently not."

"She wanted to have a literary life, and she didn't really want to go to school to find that," Debbie said. "So we had a problem, because

> *Movies must be one of the few businesses where personal pain makes you more valuable.*
>
> —DEBBIE REYNOLDS

I insisted that Carrie finish her education. Now she thanks me. But that cost me three years of not talking to my daughter. That's life."

Debbie's 1960 marriage to shoe king Harry Karl had given the family a sense of stability, but it proved to be temporary. Despite his wealth, Harry was a big gambler and brazen philanderer prone to making bad investments. "A lot of Carrie's problems started in 1972 when my husband lost all the money and the homes and the cars and everything we had," Debbie said.

Carrie struggled to cope with the challenges her mother faced. "During my adolescence, I found out that my mother was human. She had problems. This was not all right with me," Carrie remembered. "Her world was supposed to revolve around me. Her having difficulties couldn't have come at a more difficult time. Couldn't she have scheduled all her messes to come after I left home?"

## THE FORCE

Growing up in the shadow of Debbie Reynolds was not always easy. "She was this movie star, she had that inner light, she glowed from within," Carrie said. "There was something in me that wasn't happening. I wasn't from that ilk."

George Lucas disagreed. After only a small role in the film *Shampoo*, she was cast by Lucas as the sassy and self-confident Princess Leia in the wildly popular film *Star Wars*. At just nineteen, Carrie had become an overnight sensation and an internationally known star. "I didn't want to go into acting," Carrie said, "but if the people I was hanging around with had been grocers, I would have gone into food marketing."

The ensuing space trilogy—*Star Wars, The Empire Strikes Back* and *Return of the Jedi*—earned her more than one million dollars. Carrie would go on to appear in such hyper-hip fare as *The Blues Brothers, Hannah and Her Sisters, Amazon Women on the Moon* and *When Harry Met Sally*. But the road ahead had plenty of twists and turns to keep things interesting.

# That's What Friends Are For

In the world of Hollywood, where relationships tend to last only as long as there is something to be gained, Carrie Fisher is famous for her friendships. Running the gamut from writers to directors, producers to actors, it seems that everyone she meets quickly becomes a close friend and stays that way. Penny Marshall has called her a best friend since 1968 and is godmother to her daughter, Billie. Every October, Penny and Carrie cohost their joint birthday party. Carrie is still close with Meryl Streep, who played her in the movie version of her novel *Postcards from the Edge*. Yet maintaining an extraordinary number of long, genuine friendships is not always easy. When actress Joan Hackett was dying of ovarian cancer, columnist Liz Smith reported that Carrie paid the hospital bills. When a friend was stricken by AIDS, Carrie moved him into her home to care for him. The illustrious list of other friendly names includes Richard Dreyfuss, Salman Rushdie, Marianne Faithfull, Irish host Graham Norton, Meg Ryan, Craig Bierko, Tracey Ullman, Griffin Dunne, Dr. Arnold Klein, David Geffen, Ed Begley Jr., Helen Fielding, Michael Tolkin, Bruce Wagner, Ruby Wax, David Mirkin and producer Bruce Cohen.

# FAST TIMES

Sometime in the 1970s, Carrie had begun to use cocaine, which eventually led to an addiction. By 1980, she was getting friendly with Dan Aykroyd and John Belushi during the filming of *The Blues Brothers*. They were known for their outrageous humor and hearty appetite for drugs, and Carrie's partying ways spun even further out of control. In fact, she has said that she was stoned for the entire filming of her next movie, *Under the Rainbow*.

"Why drugs? They were there," Carrie noted. "I wanted to be accepted by people who did drugs. I thought I was too excited. I had this energy. Call it manic. Drugs put me where I perceived everyone else to be. They made me relax."

When John Belushi famously overdosed and died in 1982, surely it slowed Carrie down. But not for long. In 1985, at just twenty-eight, she woke up in a hospital bed after having her stomach pumped. She had been brought in for an overdose of cocaine and Percodan. (At one point she was taking as many as thirty Percodan a day.) She entered rehab and spent the next year working the Twelve Step Program.

Her visit to rehab also brought about the diagnosis of bipolar illness, also called manic depression. While she had reportedly been diagnosed as a teenager and again at twenty-

*The scariest thing Belushi ever said to me was, "You're like me." And then he died.*

—CARRIE FISHER

four, it was not something she was willing to believe. "I had a doctor tell me I was hypomanic," Carrie said. "He said I should go on lithium. I didn't believe him. I thought he was trying to get rid of me." Then she had a psychotic break and had to be hospitalized. At the time, the one person she could

not bear to face was her mother. Remarkably, she asked her not to visit.

Today Carrie has taken her struggle as a charge to help change the stigma connected to mental illness. As an outspoken advocate for those with mental illness, she shares her story and tries to help people understand not only the experience, but also the fact that having such an illness need not make you a victim.

After the rocky road that was Carrie's adolescence and early adult years, Debbie and Carrie found their way back to a peaceful place. "It took years for me to be confronted with my own flaws," Carrie noted. "And in order to forgive myself those, or even to admit to having them, I had to forgive my mother for being less than perfect. I began the long road of repairing our relationship."

"She has grown intellectually and emotionally and today she is a wise, giving, deeply loving daughter and friend," Debbie said. "The chasm that existed between us is now, thankfully, a meadowland of conversation and love."

"Edith Head was one of the people I loved most in the world. She was friend, confidante, and was always there for me, like 'another mother.' … She was wildly funny and totally giving—and she was so wise. She looked at all the craziness of Hollywood behind those dark glasses of hers with a most *lovely sense of ironic sanity.* She had a very practical way of putting panic into its proper perspective, and always made you end up laughing."

—ELIZABETH TAYLOR

# HEARTS AND BONES

When Carrie met Paul Simon in 1978, she knew it was love. The relationship was known to be somewhat chaotic, but the on-again, off-again couple (she was engaged to Dan Aykroyd in 1980) remained together for seven years and married in 1983. Unfortunately, the marriage lasted only nine months.

"The bad thing about my relationship with Paul was that we were similar animals," Carrie said. "Where there should be a flower and a gardener, we were two flowers. In the bright sun. Wilting." She jokingly claims that he left her with an acoustic guitar and nine songs about her. Perhaps his most poignant being "Hearts and Bones."

It would be another seven years before Carrie would have her next significant relationship, with uber-agent Bryan Lourd. Together they had a daughter, Billie. But it wasn't long before Bryan announced that their relationship was over. What Carrie didn't know at the time was that he had fallen for someone else. Someone named Scott.

"It was not, 'I'm leaving and I'm gay, nice talkin' to ya.' It was, 'I'm leaving,' " Carrie remembered. "And I was wearing blue shorts with lobsters on them. That's all I can really tell you about the day. If I had known it was going to happen, I would have worn a better outfit.

"I did not want my daughter to grow up without a father, because that really did impact me in a significant way," Carrie said. "And affected me in my relationships with men and my ability to trust." Not only do Carrie and Bryan share custody, but they also continue to take trips together.

Carrie was thrust into an all too familiar role—single, working mother. Just like her mom before her. "Having a daughter of my own made me realize what my mother had been up against while raising me. . . . It turns out I have lived long enough not only to have a mother but to be a mother," Carrie noted. "It would also appear that not only do I have a celebrity mother, I am a celebrity mother. And there's very little I can do about any of this but enjoy it."

*One loyal friend is worth ten thousand relatives.*

*Euripides*

# Blythe Danner and Gwyneth Paltrow

Walking home one night with her producer, Bruce Paltrow, Blythe Danner stopped in to see a fortune-teller on a lark. The prophecy: The two would marry. Of course, they had to start dating first. They would go on to have two children—Gwyneth and Jake—and build equally distinguished careers. Balancing the two was not always easy. (Gwyneth used to sneak out, leaving a note on her bed in case she got caught: "Dear Mom and Dad, I didn't run away. I haven't been kidnapped. I'm

out at the clubs. You can punish me in the morning.") Gwyneth would go on to become a Hollywood darling. Her mother cites her 1999 Oscar win for Best Actress for her role in *Shakespeare in Love* as one of her proudest moments. Onstage, her mother was the first person Gwyneth thanked. Six days after celebrating Gwyneth's thirtieth birthday, her father passed away from lung cancer. Still quietly grieving, Blythe and Gwyneth took on the big screen together in the 2003 dark film *Sylvia*, playing mother and daughter. Soon after, Gwyneth married Coldplay front man Chris Martin. And then there was daughter Apple and son Moses. With a similar affable elegance, Blythe and Gwyneth have grown closer through the trials and triumphs. They believe in putting family first, especially when it comes to each other. "My daughter is a huge movie star, married to a rock star," Blythe said, "and their lives are just . . . I can't quite imagine what their lives are like. I see them all the time, but I see them as my children. I don't see them functioning as big stars."

## LAS VEGAS

In 1984, Debbie married for a third time, to real estate developer Richard Hamlett. Together, they purchased a hotel and casino in Las Vegas and developed a plan to create a Hollywood memorabilia museum with the pieces she had begun collecting in 1970. When it opened in 1993, the collection included items such as Julie Andrews's jumper and famous guitar used in *The Sound of Music*, a Betty Grable bathing suit, Marilyn Monroe's subway dress and Judy Garland's ruby slippers from *The Wizard of Oz*.

By 1996, it was clear that the dream was not to stay a reality and the couple divorced. In 1997, Debbie was forced to file for bankruptcy. Once again, she was faced with financial ruin and life on her own. "I'm not one to advise about marriage," Debbie said. "I should see a board of directors who should vote on who I should date."

*I don't believe in taking down other people. That's what I learned from my mother. I believe in loyalty and a good sense of humor and kindness.*

—CARRIE FISHER

Still the trials and tribulations only served to bring the two women closer together. "If you go down with the blow, you are out for the count," Debbie said. "I want to go out fighting. I can't say in my personal life it's been easy on me or my children. We've had to fight the whole way. That doesn't mean you can't have a good time within the fight."

# NOVEL INSPIRATION

"From the time I was eleven I wrote," Carrie said. "They had these Kahlil Gibran journals and I would fill them thinking 'someone might read this.' But I didn't dare to be a writer as a career. There's no precedent in my family. I was expected to go into show business. But more than anything else I wanted to be articulate and smart."

Arguably the queen of the semi-autobiographical novels, Carrie writes about characters who deal with drug addiction, fame, bipolar illness and divorce—with a surprising candor and wit. "It's very cathartic for me when I can write about whatever's happened. I'm a warhorse; if I have a situation that's bad, I can handle it. But I can handle it best when I joke about it. That's my writing."

Her first novel, *Postcards from the Edge,* won her a Los Angeles Pen Award for Best First Novel in 1987. While the premise is a dysfunctional mother/daughter relationship—the daughter a recently detoxed movie star who has been forced to live with her mother, a former star who has become a vehement drinker—Carrie promises that her characters are not as true to life as you might think. "My mother is totally sweet, loyal and hilarious, and if I thought I was being mean about her in the book I'd kill myself," Carrie said. "She's a true eccentric,

> Our relationship, I guess, is more interesting than most of the relationships we have with other people.
>
> —CARRIE FISHER

"I have the same friends I've had since I was a little girl. Celebrity is not a factor in our friendship. They are *real and not afraid* to contradict me, which is an extremely positive thing."

—GWYNETH PALTROW

but she has real character. You have to respect a woman who had to do everything for my brother and me."

Her family does inspire her work, though. "My grandmother really says things like, 'colder than a well-digger's butt' and 'higher than a cat's back' and 'we're not rich enough to have your problems,'" Carrie said. "It's like she's studying to be a colorful character."

Three other novels have been published so far. *Surrender the Pink,* loosely based on her short-lived marriage to Paul Simon, *Delusions of Grandma,* chronicling the birth of a child and the breakup of her relationship with Bryan Lourd, and *The Best Awful*, about struggling with bipolar disorder.

Her other writing accomplishments include working as a script doctor, and her autobiographical one-woman show entitled *Wishful Drinking*. In an oft-repeated line, Carrie sums it all up by saying, "If my life weren't funny, it would just be true. And that is unacceptable."

# THE FISHER KING

Eddie Fisher left when she was barely two years old, so Carrie felt as though she grew up without a father. They do not see each other very often and he did some very hurtful things—not the least of which was his 1984 autobiography entitled *Eddie: My Life, My Loves.*

"He wrote a beautiful book about every woman he'd ostensibly slept with—what the sex was like, what their bodies were like, if he did or didn't love them. . . . He said he didn't love my mother. It was just unnecessary and it was hurtful to people. This book came out and I said I was going to have my DNA fumigated."

There is another reason Carrie may to want to fumigate her DNA. She believes her father is an undiagnosed manic-depressive, the same hereditary disorder that she struggles with. "He bought 200 suits in Hong Kong, was married six times, and bankrupt four. It's crazy," Carrie noted. "When you are in a room with him, you are the greatest thing he's ever met; you're so amazingly HOT and FUNNY and SMART. And then he could walk into the hallway and see a jacket he likes and he wouldn't remember even having run into you."

But getting older has brought her acceptance and wisdom. "I'm too old

*We get closer and closer all the time. . . . I didn't bother turning into my mother: we just fused together.*

—CARRIE FISHER

140

to believe you get to point the finger," Carrie said. "Blame is an unfortunate feeling to harbor. You read books like *Mommie Dearest* and you can see clearly why the author had a stroke in her 40s." Perhaps the most telling note on Carrie's relationship with her father is this: She buys her mother a gift to celebrate both Mother's Day and Father's Day.

*S*he's better
than the mother
I deserve.

—CARRIE FISHER

## LIKE MOTHER, LIKE DAUGHTER

Debbie is still well known for *The Unsinkable Molly Brown*, a role she made famous. Yet surviving while maintaining a sense of humor seems to be in the genes. When asked whether or not she has a lot in common with her mom, Carrie said, "I'm different in a lot of ways. I was always very bookish, sort of an intellectual. I thought too much, and I was way too hard on myself. But I ended up being like her in a way that I never would have expected, which is that survivor thing.

"What's weird is that if you're a survivor, then what you need to do is keep creating drama in your life to show off your gift," Carrie noted. "She had the bad-relationship thing, and I had my drug problems."

Today Carrie lives in Beverly Hills in an oversize house she purchased with Bryan Lourd. It was once inhabited by Bette Davis and by costumer Edith Head. When the smaller bungalow-style house that sits just up the driveway became available, Carrie knew just whom to call.

"She said, 'Mother, the man just died,'" Debbie remembered. "And I said, 'Should I go to the funeral,' and she said, 'No, you should buy the house.'" Debbie jumped at the chance to be closer to her

*My mother does everything that she says she's gonna do. I can always call my mother, and she will take care of me. She's very sweet to me. She will bring me soup—that other people make, but still I can always rely on my mother.*

—CARRIE FISHER

"I've known her since she was just a teenager, and I really haven't seen much change in the person herself, except a growth in character. But she has always been the same person—*true and real*—and like all great beauties she becomes more so as she ages. She has had many battles to fight in her life and has won with dignity and humanity. I admire her."

—AVA GARDNER
ON ELIZABETH TAYLOR

*Becoming a mother was . . . very intimidating. I mean, I didn't know whether I would be good at it at all. . . . When I held her, I thought I would drop her. When she slept, I thought I would lose her. I loved the smell of her, loved the way her fair hair swirled into a circle at the back of her tiny head. I would watch her all the time. Who would she turn out to be? I called this watching BTV. Baby TV.*

—CARRIE FISHER

daughter and granddaughter. They have been neighbors ever since.

The advantages of living so nearby are many, not the least of which is that three women from three generations now make up a strong, caring matriarchy. These days Carrie strives to be a more conventional parent—writing instead of acting so she can be home and cooking meals so that her daughter will have memories of her in the kitchen. "I know my daughter. I major in Billie Catherine. I know her smell, what food she likes, what clothes she wears, what cartoons she watches, that she likes Austin Powers, dogs, Rugrats, Christina Aguilera, pizza, vanilla ice cream, and that her favorite color is blue," Carrie noted. "On the other hand I know my mother likes old movies, guacamole, molasses chips from See's Candies, silver picture frames, reading gossip magazines, popcorn, German Rhine wine and the color green, like her eyes." In the end, we learn who we love.

The close proximity also gives grandmother and granddaughter plenty of time to bond. "My daughter thinks my mother is funny, because she does impersonations for her," Carrie said. "They're very blond together. My daughter is a natural blond, and my mother is by bottle, so they look alike. My mother was very athletic, and my kid is sort of athletic. That skipped a generation, because I'm the chick with the book in the room."

And while both Carrie and Debbie hope that Billie never has to face some of the things they have faced together, one hopes she is prepared to go up against two fierce women who are sure to be her best friends and role models. "My mother was always my grandmother's little girl. She became her little girl whenever they were together," Carrie said. "In the same way, I will always be the child I was to my mother, and Billie will always, in some way, be a child to me. It's difficult to believe that your children can function well, if at all, without your direction. You get so used to guiding them. What is the cutoff age for all this? As it turns out . . . Never."

Lauren Bacall
and Katharine Hepburn

# Chapter Six

# FRIENDS ARE
# TIMELESS

ello, Dexter' (spoken warily). 'Hello, George' (spoken disapprovingly). 'Hello, Mike' (spoken breathlessly). Only one voice does one hear—only one face does one see. It could never be otherwise.

"I was 15, sitting in a 55-cent balcony seat at the Shubert Theater on Broadway when I heard those words and saw the face of Katharine Hepburn live for the first time," Lauren recalled. "It was *The Philadelphia Story*. I knew then that she was different. She is that rare creature, her voice immediately bringing to mind her astonishing face. She is a member of that club of very few actresses who at their sound are totally identifiable. An immediate vision . . . Katharine Hepburn that afternoon made me glad to be alive—and sure that being an actress was the *only* goal in life."

By the time they met, Lauren Bacall (Betty to her friends) and Katharine Hepburn (Kate, Katie or even Auntie Katie) were already known as the better halves of two of Hollywood's best-known on-screen and offscreen couples—Hepburn and Tracy and Bogart and Bacall. It would be the on-screen pairing of Bogart and Hepburn for John Huston's *The African Queen* that would bring them together. From the bonds begun in Africa came a lifetime of friendship. Lauren and Katharine supported each other as two of the early feminists in Hollywood who went on to become icons—both in style and in the ways of the modern-day woman. Despite a nearly seventeen-year age difference, these two friends would survive fifty years of career ups and downs, lost loves and life as independent women alone in the world.

# HEPBURN AND TRACY

Katharine met Spencer Tracy on the set of *Woman of the Year* (1942). She was a three-time nominated, one-time winner of the Oscar. He was a three-time nominated, two-time winner. At their first meeting, clad in high heels, she said, "I'm afraid I'm a bit tall for you, Mr. Tracy." To which producer Joseph L. Mankiewicz responded, "Don't worry, Kate, he'll cut you down to size."

She was coming off a five-year relationship with Howard Hughes. Spencer Tracy was seven years her senior. A known rabble-rouser who was prone to having affairs, he also battled alcoholism. He was married, albeit unhappily. This was not a problem since Katharine, who had been married once before, professed to not be the marrying kind. Though he would eventually separate from his wife, he would never divorce, because he was a Roman Catholic. He was one of the few to call her Kathy.

They would make nine movies together, most notably *Woman of the Year*, *State of the Union* (1948), *Adam's Rib* (1949), *Pat and Mike* (1952), *Desk Set* (1957) and *Guess Who's Coming to Dinner* (1967).

"Onscreen Spencer and I are the perfect American couple," Katharine noted. "I needle him. I irritate him. I try to get around him. If he put a big paw on my head, he could squash me. I think this is the romantic, ideal picture of the male and female in this country."

We loved them on-screen while offscreen they loved each other. "What Spencer saw in me I'll never know," she says. "He thought me rather peculiar, of ambiguous sexuality and that I had dirty fingernails. . . . I do know what I saw in him— humor, intelligence, talent." Of course, Spencer also had his problems. He was a married father of two. And he drank— sometimes too much.

Though she would never understand the demons that haunted him, Katharine would prove to be the most devoted

of partners. "[He] made me understand for the first time what it really meant to be in love," she said. "There are some people that are shocked that I gave up my independence for a man, [but] it gave me pleasure to make him happy, to ease his agonies. I never felt that way about anyone before and I'm sure I never will again."

*If you want to sacrifice the admiration of many men for the criticism of one, go ahead, get married.*

—KATHARINE HEPBURN

"She just adored him," Lauren remarked. "It was the only time that Katie stopped talking, because she was always hanging on his every word. She was like a 12-year-old girl sitting at his feet looking at him in wonder. Katie girlish was just . . . never seen anything quite like it."

"I liked the idea of being my own single self," Katharine said. "Even when I was living with Spencer Tracy and he and I were together for twenty-seven years, we never really thought about or discussed marriage. He was married and I wasn't interested."

"Spence, on his part, was always sweet with her, affectionate, though not overly demonstrative," Lauren remembered. "But there was no doubt in my mind, or anyone's who saw them together, that they were totally committed to one another and that they belonged together."

# Katharine Hepburn and Vivien Leigh

When the search for *Gone with the Wind*'s indelible Scarlett O'Hara was on, Katharine offered to fill the role as a favor to producer David O. Selznick, noting that she was not sure she had enough sex appeal to properly play the part. It was Vivien Leigh who would bring Scarlett to life. Though she was considered a risky choice—she was British and engaged in a fairly public

affair with the still married Laurence Olivier, and executives worried if the public would accept her. Accept her they did. And through it all, Katharine and Vivien became friends. Soon after, Katharine was the maid of honor at Vivien and Laurence Olivier's wedding. Reportedly, Olivier got lost on the way to the ceremony and a big fight ensued between the bride and groom in the front seat, with their friends stuck listening in the backseat. Olivier and Leigh were married for nearly twenty years and were known as "the" golden couple of English theater. Katharine and Vivien remained close friends until Vivien's death in 1967.

# Spencer Tracy and Pat O'Brien

Spencer Tracy and Pat O'Brien met at the Roman Catholic, all-male Marquette Academy in Milwaukee, Wisconsin. After a little bit of college and a stint in the navy during World War I, the pair moved to New York to attend the American Academy of Dramatic Arts. They were roommates who shared not only a bathroom, but also a suit. They could only afford one and so whoever had the audition got to wear it. They survived "on pretzels, rice and water" and the benevolence of their Irish landlady. In New York, they became friends with James Cagney, performing stock theater together. Soon the trio was joined

by actor Frank McHugh, and the Boys Club, as they called it, was born. The press dubbed them the Irish Mafia. Once a week, they would meet to share stories, laugh and occasionally weigh in on potential projects. Though some members would move west, the dinners continued through the 1950s. Both Spencer and Pat had considered joining the priesthood before settling on acting. Ironically, Spencer would portray a priest on-screen four times, Pat three. Pat would also work alongside Spencer in two movies, and alongside James Cagney in nine.

# BOGART AND BACALL

*To Have and Have Not* (1944) was Lauren's first movie—a leading role. It made her a star instantly. She starred opposite Humphrey Bogart, another native New Yorker, who had more than fifty films under his belt. She was the light to his dark. The sparks flew, both on-screen and off. Behind the scenes, he was married (for the third time) and she was twenty-five years his junior. He nicknamed her "baby."

"Three weeks into the movie, I was sitting in my dressing room. Bogie came in to say good night, and tilted my head up and gave me a kiss. He'd never done that before. He asked me for my phone number and I gave it to him. From then on I would get phone calls, occasionally at 3 A.M." In May 1945, they were wed.

They made three more movies together, including *The Big Sleep* (1946), *Dark Passage* (1947) and *Key Largo* (1948). Katharine said, "She and Bogie seemed to have the most enormous opinion of each other's charms, and when they fought, it was with the utter confidence of two cats locked deliciously in the same cage." They would have two children—a son and a daughter.

*Generally women are better than men—they have more character. I prefer men for some things, obviously, but women have a greater sense of honor and are more willing to take a chance with their lives.*

—LAUREN BACALL

"I'm not after fame and success and fortune and power. It's mostly that I want to have a good job and have good friends; that's the *good stuff* in life."

—DREW BARRYMORE

## WOMEN IN THE WILD

When Bogie was cast opposite Katharine for *The African Queen*, he insisted that Lauren accompany him on location, leaving their young son, Steve, at home with the nanny for months. Though she did not know Lauren well, no one was more pleased than Katharine.

The conditions in Africa were far from ideal. And the threats were many—heat, bugs, snakes, disease and rowdy men. Before leaving London for Africa, Katharine gave an interview and said, "It is quite a venture, this African jaunt, and thank God Lauren Bacall is coming along."

"At first, Katie seemed nervous and talked compulsively," Lauren recalled. "I concluded her talking stemmed from being a woman alone, in an inaccessible part of the world, at the mercy of Huston and Bogart, about whom she'd heard all kinds of stories, the least of which was that they drank. I thought she was apprehensive—was trying to make it appear she could handle any situation, that she knew all about men like them. As it turned out, she could—and she did."

Katharine's first impression of Lauren was somewhere between awe and jealousy. "I kept looking at her and looking at her," Katharine remembered. "In the first place, she is young and she has lovely tawny skin and she has the most fabulous sandy hair. Beautiful whether it's straight or curled. In fact you have never seen her until you have seen her in her bright green wrapper on the way to the outhouse in the early morning with her hair piled up on her head and no lipstick or anything else. Her sleepy-slanty green eyes and her common-sense look and her lost voice and her lanky figure and her apparent fund of pugilistic good-nature . . . I gazed at her and wondered whether I would go mad with jealousy as I compared our ages—our skin—our hair—our natures. No, she didn't sweat much either."

"For a woman to go out to Africa with these two crazy men; who the hell knows," Lauren said. "All through the making of *The African Queen*, we were buddies. We came back from shooting one day and went into our huts. Both of us came screaming out because the floors of our cabins were just covered with ants."

One day, Katharine had to go into the water to release *The African Queen*, which was stuck on the reeds. Fearing the crocodile-infested waters, Huston explained that he would have his men fire several shots into the water to scare off any potential predators. Katharine thought about this for a minute and said, "Yes, but what about the deaf ones?" She did it anyway.

In time, Katharine came to love Africa. Despite a persistent stomach problem, she would go big game hunting with director John Huston. She would never fire a shot, but she wanted to experience Africa with the men. "She just kept on going," Lauren

*Time with her was more than time well spent. A little bit with her was worth days and weeks and months with somebody else.*

—LAUREN BACALL

remembered. "She had nobody there with her, no assistants, no entourage, nothing. She was just Katie. Bogie had enough of Africa by the end of the shoot. Katie would be riding a bicycle, picking wildflowers. She could have stayed there for a year."

The challenges of their surroundings made Lauren and Kate instant intimates and bred a mutual respect for their independent natures and idiosyncrasies. "Once she gets on the track of anything, be it picking out a can of baked beans or doing her nails or typing a letter or sunbathing or talking to anyone," Katharine noted, "don't try to get her on anything else—don't try to hurry her—she is immovable."

"Katie is a formidable woman, no doubt about it," Lauren said. "We kid each other about being difficult. I mean, we both are. She is very demanding and has no patience with anything but the best. Neither do I. She can be very abrupt and say things quite bluntly at times. I do the same thing."

## FASHION FORWARD

Lauren, who started as a model, became a fashion icon for the 1940s glamour and the embodiment of the modern-day woman. Her husky voice and sultry looks were ideals to strive for, preferably wrapped up in satin.

In contrast, Katharine never strayed far from her own inimitable style. She was prone to slacks and no makeup, a far cry from the glamour Hollywood usually demanded. "She always had a big straw hat keeping the sun off her face and a torn shirt," Lauren noted. "George Cukor used to always say, 'You think that Katie has no clothes.' You don't understand that she has a closet full of khaki pants and shirts all custom-made. You know, she was never a fashion maven; she was just a natural. She believed in comfort."

A by-product of her active, sports-loving persona, which included a loathing for skirts and dresses, Katharine's clothes were practical for any occasion. Though she did not normally attend awards shows, the one time she graced the Academy Awards, she did it in a simple black suit and flats.

"I realized long ago that skirts are hopeless," she wrote. "Anytime I hear a man say he prefers a woman in a skirt, I say: 'Try one. Try a skirt.'" Although her choices were based on comfort, her trademark trouser look became so influential that the Council of Fashion Designers of America gave her a Lifetime Achievement Award in 1985. Lauren would receive her own CFDA Fashion Icon Award in 1995.

"Anne Bancroft has the best laugh in the world. Lusty and appreciative and as delicious as a pickle right from the barrel.... As an actress, she is staggering. As a coworker, enriching. And, as a friend, God love her, Annie is as *generous and nourishing* as her wonderful laugh."

—PATRICIA NEAL

# LIVING ON

While Africa had brought them together and the years shared made them close, it was perhaps the deaths of their spouses that truly bonded them.

In 1955, Humphrey Bogart was diagnosed with cancer. Katharine and Spencer came to visit him regularly. On January 12, 1957, when it was time to leave, Katharine remembered, a special moment occurred. "Spence patted him on the shoulder and said, 'Goodnight, Bogie.' Bogie turned his eyes to Spence very quietly and with a sweet smile covered Spence's hand with his own and said, 'Goodbye, Spence.' Spence's heart stood still. He understood." Bogart died the next morning. Now a widow and mother of two, Bacall was just thirty-three years old.

Lauren asked Spencer to deliver the eulogy at the funeral. He declined, explaining that it was simply too difficult for him. Emotions were running high. *The African Queen* director and a close friend of Bogie, John Huston, delivered the eulogy instead.

"For myself, I can only say that he changed me," Bacall said. "He was my teacher, my husband, my friend. In his life and work, Bogie was integrity, truth and courage. He taught me how to live. That it was OK to trust. He taught me to keep going no matter what. He did. And he is."

After Bogie passed away, Katharine asked Lauren for one of his sweaters, which she continued to wear, mending it when need be. She invited Lauren to visit her and Spencer Tracy often. "I spent a great deal of time with them after Bogie died," Lauren noted. "Somehow, I always felt Bogie was the invisible fourth. The vision of him always came up in conversation."

*If you always do what interests you, at least one person is pleased.*

—KATHARINE HEPBURN

Ten years later and just seventeen days after completing their last film *Guess Who's Coming to Dinner*, Spencer woke in the middle of the night and decided to make some tea. When Katharine heard a teacup crash on the kitchen floor, she rushed in to find that Spencer had passed away from a heart attack. The Oscar Katharine would win for her performance was no consolation. She was devastated, but did not attend his funeral out of respect for his wife and children.

Many wondered how the two had survived so much for so long. "Love has nothing to do with what you are expecting to get—only with what you are expecting to give—which is everything," Katharine would later say. "What you will receive in return varies. But it really has no connection with what you give. You give because you love and you cannot help giving. If you are very lucky, you may be loved back. . . . I loved Spencer Tracy. He and his interests and his demands came first. This was not easy for me because I was definitely a *me me me* person. It was a unique feeling that I had for S.T. I would have done anything for him. My feelings—how can you describe them?—the door between us was always open. There were no reservations of any kind."

# Lauren Bacall and Judy Garland

When you think of the Rat Pack, rarely do women come to mind. Yet, the term Rat Pack is rumored to have been coined by Lauren Bacall or her friend Judy Garland, who met as neighbors during the 1950s. It began with Humphrey Bogart when he served as the common tie in a group of friends who frequently partied together. In one version of the story, Lauren saw this group of red-eyed, tired, drunken friends after a five-night party binge in Las Vegas and stated that they looked like a rat pack. In another version, the term came from the Holmby Hills Rat Pack, a group of friends who met on Monday nights at Judy's house to play poker. Regardless, Lauren was voted Den Mother while Judy held post as the First Vice President. "In order to qualify, one had to be addicted to nonconformity, staying up late, drinking, laughing, and not caring what anyone thought or said about us," Lauren said. When Bogart died, Frank Sinatra took over and the Rat Pack became famous as Sinatra, Dean Martin, Peter Lawford, Sammy Davis Jr. and Joey Bishop. As for Lauren and Judy, they remained close friends until Judy's death in 1969.

## SECOND CHANCES

In 1962, Katharine would star opposite Jason Robards Jr., who had recently become Lauren's second husband, in *Long Day's Journey into Night*. He would play the alcoholic brother, while she would play a morphine-addled mother of two. It was not long before Jason's real-life alcoholism would tear his marriage to Lauren apart.

*I* never realized until lately that women were supposed to be the inferior sex.

—KATHARINE HEPBURN

"While I was having problems with my second marriage, she was always there for me," Lauren recalled. "When I gave birth to Sam, my last child, I wanted her to be the godmother. She said, 'Why on earth me? I don't even like children.' She always put on this act of not caring, but she cared deeply about everyone. The day I came home from the hospital with my son, the doorbell rang and it was Katie, standing in the hallway with a bouquet of flowers in her hand."

*The glory of friendship is not the outstretched hand, nor the kindly smile, nor the joy of companionship; it is the spiritual inspiration that comes to one when he discovers that someone else believes in him and is willing to trust him with a friendship.*

*Ralph Waldo Emerson*

# Tony, Tony, Tony

The year was 1970. At the Tony Awards, Lauren was
nominated for her role in the musical *Applause*
alongside her friend Katharine, who was nominated for
her role in *Coco*. The night before the awards ceremony, Lauren picked up the phone to find Katharine at
the other end. Katharine had a favor to ask: "When my
name is announced as the winner, would you mind
picking up my award for me?" Yet it was Lauren who
would win the statue that night. Afterward, Katharine
graciously said, "I don't feel robbed because these
things don't mean much to me.... Betty is so happy that
I can't help being happy for her." The next day, she
delivered a watercolor self-portrait she had painted just
for Lauren.

# AND THEN THERE WAS ONE

As Katharine aged, her mind began slipping away. During these times, Lauren would come to visit, sitting with her, recounting stories of their friendship, their loves and their travels. "The very last time I saw her, I walked right over to her in her chair in the living room, sat next to her, kissed her. She seemed to know me a little. There were two large picture books—one with a shot of Bogie from *The African Queen*—one of Spence. As I showed each to her and spoke to her of these two men who meant so much to her, she miraculously seemed to brighten and understand."

Katharine would pass away in 2003 at the remarkable age of ninety-six. "Remembering the 15-year-old me in the third balcony watching her on stage in *The Philadelphia Story*—in complete awe—to meeting her, getting to know her, during the filming of *The African Queen* in the wilds of the Belgian Congo and the Victoria Falls, seeing the side of her few would have seen. Being accepted as a true friend, despite the difference in our ages—with our bond growing stronger through Bogie's illness

She leaves me with so many pictures of her in so many different places at so many different times. She unknowingly made me aware of ways to live and to behave that were new to me. So although there is a large, empty space in my life without her, there is all that past to remember.

—LAUREN BACALL

and death. Then the following years of closeness as we traveled for work and life in general until Spencer's death, and being able to talk about our lives on a personal level—to her arriving at my apartment with a small bouquet of flowers in her hand a few hours after I brought my newborn son, Sam, home from the hospital—the first of my friends to set eyes on him—his godmother.

"Until the day she died, I never thought of Kate without thinking of Spence and Bogie. After all, our friendship really began and solidified during the making of *African Queen* in 1951. To think that Kate's and my friendship endured for more than 50 years is some kind of record. And it created a special bond

*I* think friendship
is the most valuable
relationship you can
have in your life.
—LAUREN BACALL

*As a woman, she had made a powerful impact on all who didn't know her. She was independent. She chose her way of life—hurting no one and never vying for approval.*

—LAUREN BACALL

between us—me without Bogie, followed by her without Spence. Those years of memories of four of us—then three of us—then two of us. Now, only one."

In 1981, Lauren would reprise Katharine's role in *Woman of the Year* onstage, winning a Tony Award. In 2006, Lauren was chosen to receive one of the first Katharine Hepburn Medals, created by Bryn Mawr College to annually "recognize women whose lives, work and contributions embody the intelligence, drive and independence of the four-time Oscar-winning actress."

# Acknowledgments

*F*irst, it is important to thank all of the friends in this book who share themselves so well with the world. There are so many unique talents represented who entertain, thrill and inspire us. Thank you.

At Dutton Books, my wise guide, editor and luckily also my friend, Julie Doughty. Without your good nature and ability to laugh when things get tough, I would be bereft. Also a special nod of gratitude to Lily Kosner, who jumped in to save the day just when it was needed. Thank goodness for you. And last, but never least, Stacy Noble, without whom you likely would have never heard of this little book.

A raised glass for Chris Calhoun, my champion and favorite bonus pop partner. I will never tire of you calling me "kid."

Thank you also to Cecelia Mendes at AKG Images, Beth Jacques at MPTV, Larry Van Cassele at Getty Images, Neal Peters and David Smith at The Neal Peters Collection and Norman Currie at Corbis for all of their help in securing the wonderful photos that make the subjects in this book sing.

A sincere debt of gratitude is owed to all of the biographers, interviewers, journalists and documentarians who covered their subjects so well. Without you, we would know so much less.

This book is also for my friends. Whether we are laughing or crying, I am always glad that we are in it together.

# Sources

**ARTICLES**

"Borderland of Bohemia: Misia and The Muses," *Time*, November 9, 1953.

"Marlon and Wally," *Los Angeles Times / Weekend Standard*, November 6–7, 2004.

"Remembering Marlon Brando," The Associated Press, CBS News, September 22, 2004.

Andrews, Julie. "My Friend Carol Burnett," *Good Housekeeping*, January 1972.

Backer, Kym Allison. "Vivica A. Fox: Real Simple," *Upscale Magazine*, April 2008.

Brockes, Emma. "Carrie Fisher: Get Me to the Funny Bar," *The Guardian*, February 16, 2004.

Brownmiller, Susan. "The Unsinkable Debbie Reynolds," *The Washington Post*, October 9, 1988.

Burnett, Carol. "My Friend Julie Andrews," *Good Housekeeping*, 1963.

DiStefano, Blase. "Reynolds Wrap," *OutSmart Magazine*, August 1998.

Dullea, Georgia. "At Lunch With: Blythe Danner and Gwyneth Paltrow; Not Entirely Out of Character," *The New York Times*, August 3, 1994.

Evans, David. "Debbie Reynolds, Vegas Hotel File Chapter 11," *Bloomberg News, Rocky Mountain News* (Denver, CO), July 8, 1997.

Eyre, Hermione. "The Interview: Carrie Fisher," *The Independent*, February 22, 2004.

Fisher, Carrie. "Debbie Reynolds chats with daughter Carrie Fisher," *Good Housekeeping*, February 1, 1997.

Fisher, Carrie. "Friends, lovers, facialists . . . editing your address book can be satisfying, sentimental and saddening all at once. Here, Carrie Fisher takes us on her own trip through the pages of her little black book," *Harper's Bazaar*, January 1, 2005.

Foxley, David. "Blythe Danner: I Want to Be Part of It—New York, New York," *The New York Observer*, January 4, 2008.

Gross, Michael. "Carrie Fisher, Novelist, Looks Back at the Edge," *The New York Times*, August 14, 1987.

Hensley, Dennis. "Sex, drugs, gay men, and Carrie Fisher: the unsinkable actress-author, whose gay superagent husband left her for another man, talks about getting it all down on paper in her funny and forgiving new novel," *The Advocate*, February 3, 2004.

Holden, Anthony. "Sneak Previews of Forthcoming Books of Special Interest to Southern Californians, Secretly Married," *Los Angeles Times Magazine*, September 18, 1988.

Janos, Leo. "The Private World of Marlon Brando," *Time*, May 24, 1976.

Kane, George. "The unsinkable spirit of Debbie Reynolds / Actress and her daughter survive star wars," *Colorado Springs Gazette Telegraph*, July 14, 1989.

Keller, Julia. "Hypertext: Reading Between the Links," *Chicago Tribune*, August 15, 1999.

Klugman, Jack. "Jack Klugman on Friendship and Politics," *ABC News This Week with George Stephanopoulos*, November 13, 2005.

Lagattuta, Bill. "The Unsinkable Debbie Reynolds Still Performing After All These Years," *CBS News*, December 28, 2000.

LoBianco, Lorraine. "Spencer Tracy Profile," tcm.com.

Luscombe, Belinda. "Manchild Has Boy Child," *Time*, February 24, 1997.

Ma, Lybi. "Interview: The Fisher Queen," *Psychology Today*, November/December 2001.

Marshall, Penny. "Penny Marshall marshals her wits and fishes for dish with Carrie Fisher," *Interview*, May 1, 1994.

Morden, Darryl. "Taylor, King Revisit Early Days in L.A.," *Billboard*, November 30, 2007.

Morgan, Piers. "Interview: Michael Jackson," *The Daily Mirror*, April 1999.

Owens, Mitchell. "A Muse with a Vision of Her Own, Built on Crystal," *The New York Times*, January 3, 1999.

Pedersen, Erik. "James Taylor, Carole King weave new tapestry," Reuters, November 29, 2007.

Spada, James. "The Unsinkable Debbie Reynolds," *McCall's*, March 1997.

Sternbergh, Adam. "Blythe Danner's real (Gwyneth) and pretend (vodka) motherhood," *New York Magazine*, March 26, 2006.

Thomas, Bob. "Debbie Reynolds Remains Unsinkable," debbiereynolds online.com, November 29, 2001.

Wayne, George. "A New Debbie Dawning: Debbie Reynolds and Her Maternal Flame," *Vanity Fair*, February 1997.

Wayne, George. "The Princess Diaries: Carrie Fisher on drugs, a failed marriage, and how she really got to wear those buns," *Vanity Fair*, November 2006.

Wild, David. "James Taylor and Carole King Return in High Style to the Troubadour," *Rolling Stone*, November 29, 2007.

Wolf, Jeanne. Carrie Fisher *(Interview)*. *Redbook*, March 1, 2001.

## BIBLIOGRAPHY

Altman, Billy. *Laughter's Gentle Soul: The Life of Robert Benchley* (New York: W. W. Norton, 1997)

Andersen, Christopher P. *An Affair to Remember: The Remarkable Love Story of Katharine Hepburn and Spencer Tracy* (New York: William Morrow and Co., 1997)

Andrews, Julie. *Home: A Memoir of My Early Years* (New York: Hyperion, 2008)

Bacall, Lauren. *Lauren Bacall By Myself* (New York: Knopf, 1978)

Bacall, Lauren. *Now* (New York: Knopf 1994)

Bacall, Lauren. *By Myself and Then Some* (New York: Harper Entertainment, 2005)

Ball, Lucille. *Love, Lucy* (New York: G.P. Putnam's Sons, 1996)

Baker, Jean-Claude and Chris Chase. *Josephine: The Hungry Heart* (New York: Cooper Square Press distributed by National Book Network, 2001)

Baker, Josephine and Jo Buillon. *Josephine* (New York: Paragon House, 1988, 1977)

Baudot, Francois. *Chanel* (New York: Universe/Vendome, 1996)

Berg, A. Scott. *Kate Remembered* (New York: G.P. Putnam's Sons, 2003)

Brady, Kathleen. *Lucille: The Life of Lucille Ball* (New York: Hyperion, 1994)

Brochu, Jim. *Lucy in the Afternoon: An Intimate Memoir of Lucille Ball* (New York: William Morrow, 1990)

Burnett, Carol. *One More Time: A Memoir by Carol Burnett* (New York: Random House, 1986)

Carlyle, John. *Under the Rainbow: An Intimate Memoir of Judy Garland, Rock Hudson and My Life in Old Hollywood* (New York [Berkeley, CA.]: Carroll & Graf Publishers, 2006)

Castelluccio, Frank. *The Other Side of Ethel Mertz: The Life Story of Vivian Vance* (Manchester, CT: Knowledge, Ideas & Trends, 1998)

Charles-Roux, Edmonde. *Chanel and Her World: Friends, Fashion and Fame* (London: Thames & Hudson, 2005)

Clarke, Gerald. *Get Happy: The Life of Judy Garland* (New York: Random House, 2000)

Davidson, Bill. *Spencer Tracy: Tragic Idol* (New York: Dutton Adult, 1988)

Edelman, Rob. *Meet the Mertzes: The Life Stories of I Love Lucy's Other Couple* (Los Angeles [New York]: Renaissance Books, 1999)

Galante, Pierre. *Mademoiselle Chanel* (Chicago: H. Regnery Co., 1973)

Gold, Arthur and Robert Fizdale. *Misia: Life of Misia Sert* (New York: Vintage Books, 1992)

Haney, Lynn. *Naked at the Feast: A Biography of Josephine Baker* (New York: Dodd, Mead, 1981)

Harris, Warren G. *Sophia Loren: A Biography* (New York: Simon & Schuster, 1998)

Hellstern, Melissa. *How to Be Lovely: The Audrey Hepburn Way of Life* (New York: Dutton Books, 2003)

Hepburn, Katharine. *The Making of The African Queen, or, How I Went to Africa with Bogart, Bacall, and Huston and Almost Lost My Mind* (New York: Knopf, 1987)

Hepburn, Katharine. *Me: Stories of My Life* (New York: Knopf, 1991)

Higham, Charles. *Lucy: The Life of Lucille Ball* (New York: St. Martin's Press, 1986)

Higham, Charles. *Kate: The Life of Katharine Hepburn* (New York: Norton, 2004)

Horowitz, Susan. *Queens of Comedy: Lucille Ball, Phyllis Diller, Carol Burnett, Joan Rivers, and the New Generation of Funny Women* (Amsterdam: Gordon and Breach, 1997)

Hotchner, A. E. *Sophia, Living and Loving: Her Own Story* (New York: William Morrow, 1979)

Jules-Rosette, Bennetta. *Josephine Baker in Art and Life: The Icon and the Image* (Urbana: University of Illinois Press, 2007)

Kanfer, Stefan. *Ball of Fire: The Tumultuous Life and Comic Art of Lucille Ball* (New York: Knopf, 2003)

Leaming, Barbara. *Katharine Hepburn* (New York: Crown Publishers, 1995)

Leigh, Wendy. *True Grace: The Life and Times of an American Princess* (New York: Thomas Dunne Books, 2007)

Levy, Alan. *Forever, Sophia: An Intimate Portrait* (New York: St. Martin's Press, 1986)

Leymarie, Jean. *Chanel* (New York: Skira/Rizzoli, 1987)

Loren, Sophia. *In the Kitchen with Love* (New York, Doubleday, 1972)

Loren, Sophia. *Sophia Loren's Recipes and Memories* (New York: GT Publishing, 1998)

Loren, Sophia. *Women & Beauty* (New York: William Morrow, 1984)

Madsen, Axel. *Chanel: A Woman of Her Own* (New York: H. Holt, 1990)

McDowall, Roddy. *Double Exposure: A Gallery of the Celebrated with Com-

*mentary by the Equally Celebrated*, compiled and photographed by Roddy McDowall (New York: Delacorte Press, 1966)

McDowall, Roddy. *Double Exposure Take Two*, compiled and photographed by Roddy McDowall (New York: William Morrow, 1989)

McDowall, Roddy. *Double Exposure Take Three*, compiled and photographed by Roddy McDowall (New York: William Morrow, 1992)

McDowall, Roddy. *Double Exposure Take Four*, compiled and photographed by Roddy McDowall (New York: William Morrow, 1993)

Mitterand, Frederic (curator). *The Grace Kelly Years: Princess of Monaco* (Milan, Monaco, New York: Skira Editore; Grimaldi Forum Monaco; distributed in North America by Rizzoli International Publications, 2007)

Morella, Joe and Edward Z. Epstein. *Forever Lucy: The Life of Lucille Ball* (New Jersey: L. Stuart, 1986)

Morley, Sheridan and Ruth Leon. *Judy Garland: Beyond the Rainbow* (New York: Arcade Publishing, 1999)

Morley, Sheridan. *Katharine Hepburn* (Boston: Little, Brown, 1984)

Paris, Barry. *Audrey Hepburn* (New York: Putnam, 1996)

Quine, Judith Balaban. *The Bridesmaids: Grace Kelly, Princess of Monaco, and Six Intimate Friends* (New York: Weidenfeld & Nicolson, 1989)

Reynolds, Debbie and David Patrick Columbia. *Debbie—My Life* (New York: William Morrow, 1988)

Sanders, Coyne Steven and Tom Gilbert. *Desilu: The Lives of Lucille Ball and Desi Arnaz* (New York: William Morrow, 1993)

Sert, Misia. *Misia and the Muses: The Memoirs of Misia Sert* (New York: John Day Co., 1953)

Shipman, David. *Judy Garland: The Secret Life of an American Legend* (New York: Hyperion, 1993)

Tannen, Lee. *I Loved Lucy: My Friendship with Lucille Ball* (New York: St. Martin's Press, 2001)

Taraborrelli, J. Randy. *Laughing Till It Hurts: The Complete Life and Career of Carol Burnett* (New York: William Morrow, 1988)

Wallach, Janet. *Chanel Style* (New York: N. Talese, 1998)

Wayne, Jane Ellen. *Grace Kelly's Men* (New York: St. Martin's Press, 1991)

Windeler, Robert. *Julie Andrews: A Life on Stage and Screen* (New Jersey: Carol Publishing Group, 1997)

Wood, Ean. *The Josephine Baker Story* (London: Sanctuary Publishing, 2000)

## AUDIO

"The Speech Burned on Carrie Fisher's Brain," *NPR Weekend Edition Saturday*, May 21, 2005.

"Actress and Novelist Carrie Fisher," *NPR Fresh Air with Terry Gross*, WHYY, February 4, 2004.

"Carrie Fisher's Wishful Drinking," *NPR Day to Day*, November 23, 2006.

## VIDEO

Julie Andrews Edwards speaking at the *L.A. Times* Festival of Books 2007, youtube.com.

*Julie and Carol at Carnegie Hall*. New York: CBS, June 11, 1962.

*Julie and Carol at Lincoln Center*. New York: CBS, December 7, 1971.

*Julie and Carol: Together Again*. Los Angeles: CBS, December 13, 1989.

*Kennedy Center Honors: Julie Andrews*, December 26, 2001.

*Sophia: Her Own Story*. New York: Thorn EMI Video, Alex Ponti and Peter Katz, producers, 1980.

*Sophia Loren: Actress Italian Style*. New York: Twentieth Century Fox Film Corp.; A&E Television Networks, 1997.

# Photo Credits

p. 49: McCabe/Express/Getty Images

p. 53: Evan Agostini/Getty Images

p. 56: Horst P. Horst/Condé Nast Archive/Corbis

p. 57: Roland Schoor/Time & Life Pictures/Getty Images

p. 61: Sasha/Getty Images

p. 62: Peter Harholdt/Corbis

p. 64: *Misia Sert* by Pierre-Auguste Renoir/National Gallery Collection; by kind permission of the Trustees of the National Gallery, London/Corbis

p. 67: George Hoyningen-Huene/RDA/Getty Images

p. 69: Horst P. Horst/Condé Nast Archive/Corbis

p. 72: Walter Sanders/Time & Life Pictures/Getty Images

p. 75: Roland Schoor/Time & Life Pictures/Getty Images

p. 79: Michael Ochs Archives/Getty Images

p. 81: Shel Hershorn/Hulton Archive/Getty Images

p. 84: American Stock/Getty Images

p. 85: Hulton Archive/Getty Images

p. 88: Hulton Archive/Getty Images

p. 89: John Florea/Time & Life Pictures/Getty Images

p. 92: Bettmann/Corbis

p. 95: CBS Photo Archive/Getty Images

p. 96: Hulton Archive/Getty Images

pp. 98–99: CBS Photo Archive/Getty Images

p. 101: Hulton Archive/Getty Images

p. 103: Larry Miller/Bettmann/Corbis

p. 106: Mario Ruiz/Time & Life Pictures/Getty Images

p. 109: Bettmann/Corbis

p. 112: John Springer Collection/Corbis

p. 113: Murray Garrett/Getty Images

p. 116: Steve Pyke/Getty Images

p. 117: Loomis Dean/Time & Life Pictures/Getty Images

p. 121: Loomis Dean/Time & Life Pictures/Getty Images

p. 122: David Sutton/MPTV.net

p. 123: Gunther/MPTV.net

p. 126: Michael Tighe/Hulton Archive/Getty Images